INTRODUCTION TO
BRITISH
CONSTITUTIONAL LAW

FOURTH EDITION

BY

D. C. M. YARDLEY

LL.B.(BIRM.), M.A., D.PHIL.(OXON.)

*of Gray's Inn, Barrister, Fellow of
St. Edmund Hall, Oxford*

LONDON
BUTTERWORTHS
1974

ENGLAND: BUTTERWORTH & CO. (PUBLISHERS) LTD.
                LONDON: 88 KINGSWAY, WC2B 6AB

AUSTRALIA: BUTTERWORTHS PTY. LTD.
                SYDNEY: 586 PACIFIC HIGHWAY, CHATSWOOD, NSW 2067
                MELBOURNE: 343 LITTLE COLLINS STREET, 3000
                BRISBANE: 240 QUEEN STREET, 4000

CANADA: BUTTERWORTH & CO. (CANADA) LTD.
                TORONTO: 14 CURITY AVENUE, 374

NEW ZEALAND: BUTTERWORTHS OF NEW ZEALAND LTD.
                WELLINGTON: 26-28 WARING TAYLOR STREET

SOUTH AFRICA: BUTTERWORTH & CO. (SOUTH AFRICA) (PTY.) LTD.
                DURBAN: 152-154 GALE STREET

ISBN—Casebound: 0 406 69003 0
Limp: 0 406 69004 9

*Printed and bound in Great Britain by R. J. Acford Ltd., Industrial Estate,
Chichester, Sussex.*

TO
MY WIFE

PREFACE TO FOURTH EDITION

The latter part of the twentieth century appears to embrace an ever-increasing momentum of constitutional change in the United Kingdom, and for this edition it has been necessary to revise the text of the book quite extensively. I have had to take account of the following recent legislation: the Town and Country Planning Act 1968, the Administration of Justice Acts 1969 and 1970, the Synodical Government Measure 1969, the Courts Act 1971, the Immigration Act 1971, the Tribunals and Inquiries Act 1971, the Industrial Relations Act 1971, the Northern Ireland (Temporary Provisions) Act 1972, the Local Government Act 1972, the European Communities Act 1972, the Northern Ireland Assembly Act 1973, and the Northern Ireland Constitution Act 1973, although in a book of this nature it is not always necessary to refer to each statute by name wherever it impinges on the matter discussed in the text. Some of this legislation has been constitutionally far-reaching, and has caused me to re-write sections of the book on Northern Ireland, local government, the courts and Parliamentary sovereignty. The impact of the United Kingdom joining the European Communities is mainly treated in this latter section. I have also taken the opportunity to re-write completely Chapter 11 on the mainstream of administrative law, and to give it a new title. In total result there has been a modest increase in the length of the book since the last edition by four pages, but I take some heart from the fact that the increase upon the length of the First Edition is only 12 pages in a period of some 14 years.

While the permanency of the new section in this book on Northern Ireland must remain in doubt until it is seen whether the people and politicians in the province will settle down under the 1973 legislation, the Report of the Royal Commission on the Constitution (Cmnd. 5460), published at the end of October 1973, suggests that most of the rest of this book is unlikely to have to be altered in future editions to take account of any legislation following from the Report. The actual proposals for change made by the Royal Commission are almost entirely concerned with the possible introduction of devolution for Scotland and Wales, and the establishment of separate Scottish and Welsh Assemblies is recommended. The Commissioners, however, have greatly weakened the strength of their proposals by a series of substantial disagreements among themselves about the extent and identity of the devolution of powers, both legislative and executive, and by differences over their approach respectively to Scotland and Wales. Some of the Commissioners favoured the establishment of regional co-ordinating and advisory councils for England, but in other respects they have made no substantial recommendations for any changes in the Constitution of the United Kingdom. The Report was published just after I had finally passed the page proofs of this edition for the press, and it was therefore impossible for me to incorporate any references to it in the text. But in view of the lack of recommendations for change over the vast majority of the field of our constitutional law, of the disagreements among the Commissioners concerning many aspects of devolution for Scotland and Wales, and of the generally frosty welcome given to the Report by politicians of the major parties, it seems that the present brief account in this Preface amounts to quite a sufficient reference to the Report for the purposes of this edition.

In the past some reviewers have criticised me for allotting a chapter to the Church, and I have considered carefully whether I ought to follow the example of Professor Hood Phillips, in his *Constitutional and Administrative Law*, by dropping it. On the whole, however, it seems to me that a survey of constitutional institutions would be incomplete without some reference to the two "established" churches of the land. *Wade and Phillips* retains a chapter on Church and State, and there are various passages to be found in Professor de Smith's *Constitutional and Administrative Law*. I do not think the space of four pages accorded to the subject in this book to be unduly profligate.

Once more I am grateful for the comments and criticisms offered either privately or in reviews, and I have done my best to take account of them, though I have not always found it possible to agree with the points raised. I hope that those who may still disagree with any part of my approach to the writing of this book will understand that introductory books are often controversial, and that those who essay to write them are attempting a task which is in many ways harder than the writing of a specialist monograph upon some topic treated in depth. For up-to-date information on the Commonwealth I should like to thank Mrs. C. L. Bazell of the Foreign and Commonwealth Office Library and Records Department. It is hoped that Part III of the book, on The Commonwealth, is now, after the trial and error of earlier editions, in a more or less permanent form and capable in later editions of absorbing any new changes in the rapidly shifting sands of the Commonwealth. Finally, I should like to thank the staff of Butterworths, whose help and understanding have been of great assistance in easing the task of preparing this edition.

D.C.M.Y.

St. Edmund Hall,
  Oxford.

November 24th, 1973.

EXTRACT FROM PREFACE TO FIRST EDITION

The author of any new book on law should be able to justify its appearance, and that justification may be by no means apparent when the subject of the work has already occupied the attentions of writers before him. The leading text-books upon the subject of constitutional law today are of such great merit that no teacher of the subject can do better than to recommend his pupils to be guided by them. It is perhaps invidious to identify these books here, but I have in mind particularly the comprehensive work of Professor Hood Phillips and also the slightly shorter volume of Professor Wade and Mr. G. Godfrey Phillips. For further reading there are many books to be consulted—Ridges, Keir and Lawson, Dicey, Anson, Taswell Langmead, Griffith and Street, to mention but a few; and it would therefore seem that any new book in the field may be superfluous. Yet, because of the absence of any single document embodying the British Constitution, there are many tudents just embarking on their study of the subject who still finds considerable difficulty in gaining a full picture of the area of law covered by it, and they are thus at somewhat of a disadvantage when reading the works I have already mentioned. In particular they find it hard to see how the Constitutions of Commonwealth countries can have anything at all to do with the law of England, and also why the constitutional law of England, unlike other branches of English law, is usually applicable to the other parts of the United Kingdom. It is my hope that the present short work may do something to remedy this state of affairs. My intention is simply to draw a brief composite sketch of the field that any student of the subject must traverse, and to suggest the problems which exist rather than to attempt to solve them. Footnotes and authorities have been deliberately kept to the minimum. Historical material is only included where it is either still part of, or necessary for the understanding of, the modern law. At the end of each chapter, however, the reader will find a short list of recommended works which will enlighten the inquiring mind upon the details of the subject. Although it is hoped that the book is intelligible to laymen, I think that most readers will already have some acquaintance with the general principles of English law and the history of the judicial system.

This volume is therefore directed primarily towards the needs of university law students just beginning their study of constitutional law, and of students who are reading for professional examinations, such as Part I of the Bar examination. But it is also hoped that those students of other subjects who require a certain knowledge of the law of the Constitution will find the present account meets their needs.

I have been very fortunate in the encouragement and help received while preparing this book. Professor H. G. Hanbury, Fellow of All Souls College, Oxford, Professor O. Hood Phillips of the University of Birmingham and Mr. G. H. Treitel, Fellow of Magdalen College, Oxford, have all read the draft typescript, and most of the improvements incorporated thereafter have been due to their thoughtful and constructive criticism. Even where I have been unable to accept such criticism its very existence has caused me to re-examine what I had previously written with the intention of making my point a little clearer. For any faults that remain I am, of course, solely responsible, and any views expressed upon the law are mine alone. I should also like to thank the publishers for their consideration and help at all stages of the writing of this work. But most of all my debt is to my pupils. It has often appeared to me that I learn far more from them than they do from me, and it is my hope that I have been able to repay some part of that debt in writing this book.

D.C.M.Y.

St. Edmund Hall,
   Oxford.

November 27th, 1959.

TABLE OF CONTENTS

LIST OF CASES CITED

xv

LIST OF STATUTES

I.B.C.L.—B

PART I

PRINCIPLES OF
BRITISH CONSTITUTIONAL LAW

CHAPTER 1

THE NATURE OF
BRITISH CONSTITUTIONAL LAW

It is very difficult to define the term "constitutional law" as applied to the United Kingdom of Great Britain and Northern Ireland. Naturally it must be that law which is concerned with the Constitution of the country.[1] But, whereas in the great majority of the nations of the civilised world it is possible to discover a single document or bundle of documents which embody the Constitution of the country concerned, in this country there is no such guide. The provisions of our Constitution must be gleaned from among the vast mass of source-material which together forms the whole body of English, Scots and Northern Ireland law. This law is derived partly from custom, but mostly from written sources, namely reports of decided cases, statutes (which, as we shall see in Chapter 2, override any already existing legal rules which conflict with them) and occasionally the writings of jurists, though these latter are only called into account where other guidance for the courts is lacking. The scope of the law is practically unlimited, for it must cover all aspects of the relationships between the individuals and authorities throughout the country. Thus it is inevitable that there should be legal rules concerning crime, matrimonial relationships, real and personal property, conveyancing, wills, sale, civil wrongs, the status of companies,

---

[1] It is not intended to explore the meaning of the word "law" in these pages. This has been the subject of much jurisdprudential thought, for which the standard works on jurisprudence should be consulted. Suffice it to say here that law amounts to those rules which the courts of law are bound to enforce.

aeronautics and the control of health, to mention but a few topics.
But it is necessary for the constitutional lawyer to divine what, out
of the whole mass of the law of the United Kingdom, amounts to
part of the Constitution.

Professor Hood Phillips has defined the Constitution of a state
as "the system of laws, customs and conventions which define the
composition and powers of organs of the state, and regulate the
relations of the various state organs to one another and to the
private citizen."[1] It is submitted that the Constitution of any
country must comprise the fundamental structure and organisation
of that country, and that therefore constitutional law is its fundamental law, its basic, essential law, whether it be civil, criminal,
public or private, together with those rules of conduct laid down to
govern the exercise of state power by the official organs of the
state. If this postulate is accepted as of general application throughout the world, then it must be accepted for the United Kingdom.
It is thus the task of any British lawyer concerned with the
Constitution to determine which laws out of the whole body of
United Kingdom law come within the realm of constitutional law.
Since there is no United Kingdom constitutional instrument
boldly laying down the laws of the Constitution, and showing the
lawyer where the line is to be drawn, any assessment of what laws
come within the field which is the subject of this book remains
largely a matter of personal opinion. It is only rarely that a court
of law expresses any opinion on the distinction, for provided the
court is able to deduce the law applicable in a given case, it is not
often concerned to declare which branch of United Kingdom law
it may belong to in comparison with other branches. Sometimes
the true classification of a legal rule must remain a matter of doubt,
but on the other hand there are frequent occasions when the
problem is by no means insoluble. For example, it is a rule of
English law that any person who inflicts injury upon another by
reason of negligence will be liable to pay damages to that other
person, though these damages may be reduced if there has been
contributory negligence on the part of the injured person. It would
be quite possible in the future for Parliament to enact a statute to
the effect that contributory negligence should cease to be a defence
in an action for negligence, and the effect would be an alteration of

---

[1] *Constitutional and Administrative Law* (5th ed., 1973), p. 5.

one of the branches of the law of torts. But the *method* by which such change had come about (*i.e.* Parliamentary legislation) would not have been altered at all.

It is not contended that this fundamental law of the state is unalterable. It is normal in most countries that the law of the Constitution should provide within itself for the method of its own alteration. Often this is a method quite different from that employed when altering or repealing laws which do not form part of the Constitution. To give but one example,[1] the constitutional document of the United States of America provides that any amendment of the Constitution may be carried out either by (1) initiation of at least two-thirds of each House of Congress, and ratification by a majority in the legislatures of at least three-quarters of the States, or by (2) initiation of a convention called on the application of the legislatures of at least two-thirds of the States, and ratification by conventions in at least three-quarters of the States, provided in either case that no State, without its own consent, may be deprived of its equal representation in the Senate.[2] These are perhaps fairly complicated methods of change, though only the first method has ever been used, and the position is quite different in this country, where constitutional change may be brought about in the same way as any other change of the law, namely by simple Act of the United Kingdom Parliament.

In many countries the Constitution comes into being as the result of a political upheaval, as in the U.S.A., where the Constitution which came into force on March 4th, 1789, was the political result of the War of Independence. In Eastern Europe after the Second World War the new political masters of most of the Russian satellite countries were able to overthrow the previously existing Constitutions, and to impose their own will in fresh Constitutions. At all events, whatever the executive regime of a particular nation, the Constitution inevitably follows from the fact of national political independence. Any such independent country may enact its own laws, including its fundamental laws, for no machinery exists to stop it from doing so. A lawyer is not professionally concerned with politics, and must confine himself to the

---

[1] Other instances may be seen in Chapter 13, *post*, in the other independent countries of the Commonwealth.
[2] *Constitution of the United States of America*, Article V.

realms of pure law, but such law is always dependent upon political fact. Jurists have frequently studied the questions of how rules become law, how a Constitution comes into being, and who has the power legally to conceive or enact a Constitution. But these questions, with which we are not concerned here, must, it is submitted, always remain theoretical, and have little relation to the reality of state necessity and state power. Nevertheless, once a Constitution exists, the lawyer must seek to enforce it and to carry it out.

As has been stated above, United Kingdom constitutional law comprises all those laws, derived from the various sources referred to above, which are fundamental to the organisation of the state, together with such lesser rules as are laid down to facilitate the working of this organisation, but it also includes a certain element of pure convention. It must be admitted that there is here a contradiction in terms. Conventions are mentioned separately because they are not laws, and the courts are therefore not bound to enforce them. They certainly do not amount to law, but they are regarded as being of so fundamental a nature that it would be unthinkable that anyone should transgress them. Also, on the rare occasions when a constitutional convention has been flouted the result has sometimes been that the convention is made into binding law by Parliament.[1] Such conventions may come into being in various ways, but normally they are said to exist because of long usage or of agreement, and because everyone is entitled to expect that they always will be followed in suitable circumstances.

Because of their practical importance, it may be suggested that constitutional conventions form the very essence or basis of the British unwritten Constitution. Instances of these conventions include the rule that the Monarch will exercise his Royal Prerogative (with a few exceptions) only with the advice of his Ministers, and that the Ministers of the Crown are collectively responsible to Parliament for the acts of any one of their number in his capacity as a Minister. Other important conventions will be mentioned in the appropriate sections of this book. But it may be as well here to note the most basic convention of all, that the

---

[1] *E.g.* as happened at the time of the passing of the Parliament Act, 1911: Chapter 2, *post.*

Government must not flout the generally expressed wishes of Parliament, and that it must not impede the lawful activities of the members of the Opposition. It is because the necessary conventions have not had a chance to grow up gradually that a newly independent Commonwealth country's constitutional document, incorporating the *legal* part of the Constitution but not its spirit, may sometimes fail, and even give rise to absolutism.

English law and British constitutional law

The term "British constitutional law" is used in the title of this present chapter. Yet, as all lawyers are brought up to remember, English law and Scots law are quite different bodies of rules, with distinct traditions and histories, even though in certain fields they have come to bear similarities to each other. Again, the law of Northern Ireland is separate from either of these two systems, and so is that of the Isle of Man and of the Channel Islands. Only between England and Wales has a fusion of laws taken place, although the true reason from which this result followed was the subjugation of the latter country by the former in the middle ages. England, Wales and Scotland together form Great Britain; and Great Britain together with Northern Ireland forms the United Kingdom: this latter body alone is recognised as the state for international purposes. The United Kingdom together with the Isle of Man and the Channel Islands form the British Isles.[1] Each of these countries, other than England and Wales, whose laws and institutions are the same, will be dealt with separately in Chapter 7 below, but for the present it is probably enough to say, in explanation of the phrase used in the chapter heading, that the constitutional laws of England and Scotland have become substantially identical, save in rare instances, and save for nomenclature,[2] and that Northern Ireland, though in normal times maintaining its own local Parliament and executive, is nevertheless part of the one Union as far as international affairs are concerned,[3] and its laws are for the most part

---

[1] Strictly speaking the Republic of Ireland also falls geographically within the British Isles, but it is now a completely independent country and outside the Commonwealth.

[2] *E.g. MacCormick* v. *Lord Advocate*, 1953 S.C.396 (see Chapter 2, *post*); also the entirely different system of courts (see Chapter 7, *post*.)

[3] Thus, citizens of the United Kingdom all bear the same nationality and status; see Chapter 8, *post*.

similar to those of England, the powers of its local legislature and executive being subject to those wielded at Westminster. The Channel Islands and the Isle of Man preserve the independence of their laws and institutions more or less intact. The term "British constitutional law" is justified in that the principles to be stated in this book are mostly common to England, Wales and Scotland, and are often similar in Northern Ireland, while they have a particular effect upon the Isle of Man and the Channel Islands. It is this common constitutional law which is of significance when considering the home country as the centre of the Commonwealth.[1]

The subjects covered by British constitutional law

Although, as has been pointed out above, the identity of the actual rules which come within the scope of our fundamental law may be the subject of dispute, it is submitted that the following short list probably covers the field:

(1) the law concerning the composition of the national legislature and legislative powers;

(2) the law concerning the composition and functions of national government;

(3) the hierarchy and status of courts of law;

(4) the limits of personal liberty and the rights of the individual;

(5) the relationship between the executive and the individual;

(6) the law of nationality and the status of aliens;

(7) the status of certain national institutions, such as the armed forces and the Church;

(8) the relations between central and local government; and

(9) the relationship between the United Kingdom and its dependencies, and with the independent members of the Commonwealth.

It is on the basis of this list that the remainder of the book will be framed.

FURTHER READING

O. Hood Phillips, *Constitutional and Administrative Law* (5th ed., 1973).

E. C. S. Wade and G. Godfrey Phillips, *Constitutional Law* (8th ed., by E. C. S. Wade and A. W. Bradley, 1970).

---

[1] See Chapter 13, *post.*

A. V. Dicey, *Introduction to the Study of the Law of the Constitution* (10th ed., by E. C. S. Wade, 1959).
Sir W. Ivor Jennings, *The Law and the Constitution* (5th ed., 1959).
Sir W. Ivor Jennings, *The British Constitution* (5th ed., 1966).
Sir D. L. Keir and F. H. Lawson, *Cases in Constitutional Law* (5th ed., 1967).
F. H. Lawson and D. J. Bentley, *Constitutional and Administrative Law* (1961).
G. Marshall and G. C. Moodie, *Some Problems of the Constitution* (4th ed., 1967).
R. F. V. Heuston, *Essays in Constitutional Law* (2nd ed., 1964).
J. D. B. Mitchell, *Constitutional Law* (2nd ed., 1968)
G. J. Borrie, *Public Law* (2nd ed., 1970).
Geoffrey Wilson, *Cases and Materials on Constitutional and Administrative Law* (1966).
O. Hood Phillips, *Reform of the Constitution* (1970).
S. A. de Smith, *Constitutional and Administrative Law* (2nd ed., 1973).
B. Jones, *British Government Today* (1972).

CHAPTER 2

PARLIAMENT

Parliament is the legislative organ of the United Kingdom; that is, its primary function is to make laws. Obedience to these laws is obligatory upon all people who owe allegiance to the Crown and who are present within the United Kingdom.[1] In certain respects Parliament has refrained from exercising jurisdiction over Northern Ireland,[2] and also over the Channel Islands and the Isle of Man.[3] Parliament sits at Westminster, and has sometimes been known as the Imperial Parliament, as it also has the right to legislate for British dependencies and, within severe limits, for other parts of the Commonwealth.[4] Other important functions of Parliament include discussion of policy, and the surveillance of the Government. It is necessary to consider six aspects of Parliament in this chapter, namely the composition of Parliament, the duration of Parliament, the procedure for making laws, other functions of Parliament, Parliamentary privilege and the sovereignty of Parliament.

I. COMPOSITION OF PARLIAMENT

There are three component parts of Parliament, the Monarch, the House of Lords and the House of Commons. It is more usual to regard Parliament as composed of only the two Houses, which sit at Westminster, but it is strictly correct to consider all three elements as part of the whole, for no legislation can come into being without the participation of the Monarch, as will be seen

---

[1] Allegiance does not necessarily depend only upon the possession of British nationality. The concept of British nationality is now, in any case, fairly complicated, and will be explained shortly in Chapter 8, *post*. Again, allegiance does not depend only on residence, but it is sufficient in this chapter to say that allegiance may be either permanent or temporary: the whole problem will be discussed in Chapter 8.

[2] See Chapter 7, *post*.

[3] See Chapter 7, *post*.

[4] This will be explained in Chapter 13, *post*.

presently. The institution of the Monarchy itself will, however, be examined in Chapter 3 rather than in the present chapter.

The House of Lords

The House of Lords is the successor of the old *Curia Regis*, which comprised the King's advisers, but the House itself, as a gathering of all the noblemen of the land, probably stems from sometime in the thirteenth century. One great difference between the modern House of Lords and the Curia is that the latter was a feudal body, whereas feudalism now plays no part in our law or society. The membership of the House has altered comparatively little since earliest times, though there have been several recent modifications, and at present it is as follows:

A. *The Lords Temporal*, who may be subdivided into:

(1) All hereditary peers and peeresses of the realm, except Irish peers. This group does not include heirs to peerages who merely hold courtesy titles and are not in fact the head of their line.[1] Peers in their own right include dukes not of royal blood, marquesses, earls, viscounts and barons, and they currently number about 900. Under the Peerage Act, 1963, however, it is now possible for any peer to disclaim his peerage for the duration of his life, leaving his next heir to decide whether or not he also will surrender the peerage when the time comes for him to succeed to the title. The main purpose of this new function is to enable those who wish to sit in the House of Commons, if duly elected, to escape the automatic disqualification (mentioned below) which attaches to a peer. Under a Standing Order of the House of Lords a procedure has also been established whereby peers who do not wish to attend the House regularly may obtain, or even sometimes be assumed to have obtained, leave of absence. Although this cannot legally prevent a peer from sitting whenever he so desires, it does nevertheless have this practical effect, thus discouraging the occasional attendance in the legislature of noble "backwoodsmen".

(2) All life peers created by the Monarch, under the terms of the Life Peerages Act, 1958. Any man or woman may receive the rank of baron under this Act, which was passed as a step towards reform of the composition of the House. Objection may

---

[1] Irish peers, and all persons who possess courtesy titles, rather than peerages, are eligible to sit in the House of Commons, if elected: see *post*.

be raised that in fact the Government of the day may nominate its own supporters as life peers, but it seems that at present none of the major political parties are likely to abuse the power conferred by the Act, which has been used partly to boost the Labour benches in the Lords, and partly to give seats in the chamber to people eminent in divers walks of life.

(3) The eleven Lords of Appeal in Ordinary ("Law Lords"), who are life peers appointed under the terms of the Appellate Jurisdiction Act, 1876, as subsequently amended.[1]

B. *The Lords Spiritual*, who are the Archbishops of Canterbury and York, the Bishops of London, Durham and Winchester, and the twenty-one most senior other diocesan bishops of the Church of England, according to seniority of appointment. The Bishop of Sodor and Man, however, never has a seat in the House, as he is always a member of the Tynwald of the Isle of Man.[2]

There are, however, certain disqualifications which will prevent a peer from being able to take his seat in the House, although he would otherwise have been entitled to do so. These disqualifications apply to:

(1) aliens;
(2) infants, that is, peers under the age of eighteen;
(3) persons convicted of treason or arrestable offences, who have not yet served their sentence or been pardoned;
(4) members expelled by the House acting as a court of law,[3] unless pardoned; and
(5) bankrupts.

The chairman of the House of Lords is the Lord Chancellor, who is also a member of the Government, and is not therefore expected to be impartial in party matters.[4] The political parties maintain supporters in the House, each party having its Leader, but since the peers do not become members of the House by

---

[1] The Act of 1876 originally provided for the appointment of only two Lords of Appeal in Ordinary.

[2] See Chapter 7, *post*.

[3] A peer expelled by a resolution of the House of Lords acting as a legislative body cannot be excluded permanently. The judicial functions of the House will be discussed later in Chapter 4.

[4] The Lord Chancellor need not strictly be a peer, but according to modern practice he always is, even if this involves the special conferment of a peerage upon him on appointment to his office.

election as party candidates there are many peers who have no political affiliations at all. The Conservative Party has often been able to rally sufficient support to ensure a majority in any critical debate or measure, though this power has been affected by the new practice of appointing life peers, as shown above. But in any case, as we shall see when examining the functions of Parliament, party politics play a much smaller role in the Lords than in the House of Commons. In the Queen's Speech at the opening of Parliament in 1967, the Labour Government stated its intention to initiate legislation to reform the House of Lords still further, and this intention was reaffirmed in 1968, but the Parliament (No. 2) Bill, which was designed to achieve such a reform, had to be abandoned in 1969 because of determined opposition from a number of back benchers on both sides of the House of Commons.

The House of Commons

The House of Commons, sometimes known as the lower House of Parliament, is a representative assembly. Its history dates from the thirteenth century, and the methods of providing representatives to sit in the House have altered very greatly in the course of its existence, particularly as a result of the Reform Acts of the nineteenth century. Today one Member of Parliament (M.P.) is elected by universal adult suffrage in each Parliamentary constituency in the United Kingdom, and the whole of the Kingdom is divided into these constituencies according to roughly equal groups of population. There is no limit to the number of candidates who may offer themselves for election in each constituency, though each must deposit £150 with the returning officer of the constituency, and this sum will be forfeited by the candidate if he fails to poll at least one-eighth of the total votes cast. The majority of candidates belong to political parties, the most powerful of which are the Conservative, Labour and Liberal Parties, and successful candidates will support or oppose the Government party according to their affiliation. But in law a candidate's or member's affiliation to a party is ignored: his status as a Member of Parliament alone, if he is elected, is all that is recognised.[1]

---

[1] The existence of political parties is, however, apparently assumed by the terms of the Ministers of the Crown Act, 1937, and the post of Leader of the Opposition is recognised in that statute.

Anyone may "stand for Parliament", but the following persons are disqualified from sitting in the House:

(1) aliens;

(2) infants;

(3) those convicted and imprisoned for at least twelve months who have not yet served their sentences or been pardoned;

(4) certain persons suffering from mental illness;

(5) peers and peeresses in their own right, other than the holders of Irish peerages;

(6) clergy of the Church of England and the Church of Ireland, ministers of the Church of Scotland, and priests of the Roman Catholic Church. Although none of these churches is represented directly in the Commons, the Church of England is represented, as has been seen, by its bishops in the Lords. Clergy of the Church in Wales may, however, sit in the Commons as a result of the Welsh Church Act, 1914;

(7) bankrupts:

(8) anyone guilty of corrupt or illegal practices at Parliamentary elections. These terms are statutorily defined, and the consequences of disqualification are dealt with in the Representation of the People Act, 1949;

(9) judges of the Supreme Court of Judicature and the County Courts, the Recorder of London and stipendiary magistrates;

(10) civil servants, police officers and members of the armed forces on the active list;

(11) sheriffs and returning officers as regards the constituencies of which they are returning officers;

(12) members of non-Commonwealth legislatures; and

(13) holders of certain specified offices, listed in section 1 and the First Schedule of the House of Commons Disqualification Act, 1957.[1] These are usually offices of profit, but the Act also preserves the traditional method whereby an M.P. may resign from the House, namely by applying for one of the sinecure positions of Steward of the Chiltern Hundreds or of the Manor of Northstead.

---

[1] The Ministers of the Crown Act, 1964 also lays down that no more than ninety-one members may hold ministerial office.

The chairman of the House is the Speaker, who is elected from among its members by the whole House at the beginning of each Parliament. The election is often unanimous after the Government party and the Opposition have held informal discussions upon the subject[1]. The political division of the members is far more pronounced than in the House of Lords. The Government, headed by the Prime Minister, is normally formed from the party which has the largest group of members in the Commons, and which then becomes known as the Government party. The Prime Minister will appoint an influential member of this party as Leader of the House. Members of parties which oppose the Government party are then termed the Opposition, and the most powerful Opposition party will elect one of its number to be Leader of the Opposition. The support of members of either the Government or Opposition parties in any vote is ensured by means of the "Whips", who are M.P.s chosen within the party concerned, or by the Prime Minister for the Government party, to maintain party discipline and regularity of attendance at the House on important occasions. Although "Whips" also function in the House of Lords their importance is not so great there, partly because of the large number of independent members in that House, and partly because, as we shall see presently, the Lords have far less power than the House of Commons. Government "Whips" hold titular posts as Lords of the Treasury or members of the Royal Household. The strict party system in the Commons may in some measure detract from the quality of debate in that chamber, and it does tend to prevent members from voting according to conscience; but on the other hand the stability, both within the House and of the Government—for, as we shall see in the next chapter, the existence of the Government depends on the continued support of the majority in the Commons—contributes greatly to the general stability of the country, and enables the House to work through a lot of business without undue hindrance.

II. DURATION OF PARLIAMENT

Section 7 of the Parliament Act, 1911, enacts that no Parliament may last for more than five years, and unless Parliament has already been dissolved by the Monarch its life will terminate by

---

[1] The election was contested in 1951 and 1970.

lapse of time exactly five years after it came into being. A general election of members of the Commons will then be held, although the composition of the Lords will not be altered by this event. It is, however, always open to Parliament to extend its own life by means of an Act of Parliament, and this has been done, for example, during the war of 1939–1945; but it is conventional to effect this prolongation only from year to year. Casual vacancies in the Commons are filled by holding a bye-election in any constituency affected.

Each new Parliament is summoned by the Monarch, and divides its time into sessions, normally covering periods of about one year each, though they are sometimes held more frequently. Sessions are ended by the Monarch "proroguing" Parliament. The sittings of Parliament within each session are also divided up by periods of "recess".

III. Procedure for Making Laws

A law is made by the passing of a statute through Parliament. In the course of its passage it is known as a Bill, but when it is passed it becomes an Act of Parliament. Such Acts must be approved by a majority of the votes cast in each House, and then receive the assent of the Monarch. Certain exceptions to this procedure of the passage of a Bill through both Houses are provided for in the Parliament Acts, 1911 and 1949, which will be discussed later in this chapter. There are three main kinds of Bill, Public, Private and Hybrid. Public Bills concern law which will be of general application when it is passed. Private Bills are measures dealing with personal matters or local matters in a certain area of the country only. Hybrid Bills are otherwise Public Bills which nevertheless affect private interests in such a way as to render it desirable that part of the procedure for Private Bills be adapted for their passage. The procedure for the passage of each of these types of measure will be sketched in these pages, but first it should be noted that such procedure is conventional only, save where the Parliament Acts, 1911 and 1949, apply. It is within the competence of either House to vary its procedure, yet the conventional practice is unlikely to be disturbed. Bills will be either Government Bills (that is, introduced by a member of either House who is also a Minister) or Private Members' Bills

(introduced by a member of the House who is not a member of
the Government, or who is introducing the Bill purely in his
private capacity as a member of the House). Government Bills
occupy far more time in Parliament, because Parliamentary time
is allocated by the Leader of the House, and very little time is
allotted to Private Members' Bills. In fact only certain Fridays of
the year are currently set aside for this purpose, and members
wishing to introduce such Bills must ballot for the right to do so
on one of these days. It may be thought that in practice too little
time is now allowed for the consideration of Private Members'
Bills, which are often of greater importance than the time spent
on them would suggest. They do indeed provide the ordinary
citizen with the opportunity to initiate legislation which is not
necessarily of importance to the Government. Such measures were
the far-reaching Matrimonial Causes Act, 1937, introduced by
Mr. (later Sir) A. P. Herbert, and the Murder (Abolition of Death
Penalty) Act, 1965, introduced by Mr. Silverman.

A. *Public Bills*

These Bills may originate in either House, although most Bills
in fact go through the Commons before the Lords, and Money
Bills and other Bills with financial clauses may not originate in
the House of Lords, but the procedure is largely similar in both
Houses. The member introducing the Bill will either present it at
the Table of the House or, more rarely, move for leave to introduce
it.[1] In either case the member will previously have given notice of
his intention. There then follow at intervals the first and second
readings, the committee stage, the report stage and the third
reading. The first reading is purely formal, when the Clerk of the
House reads out the title of the Bill only. The second reading,
however, is the vital stage at which it is decided whether a Bill
will be defeated out of hand or will go forward for further consideration. Normally the member who introduced the Bill will speak
in its favour, pointing out the main principles involved. There is no
possibility of altering details at this stage, and the Bill must stand
or fall on its general merits. If the Bill is unopposed, then it will
be "read" a second time very quickly, but if it is opposed then a

---

[1] Private members also have the privilege of moving for leave to introduce
Bills after "Government business' on any day, but as only ten minutes are
allowed for each such introduction, plus ten minutes for any opposition, little
more than publicity is likely to result.

debate on the principles of the Bill will take place, after which a vote is taken. Of course a Government Bill is very unlikely to be defeated, but a Private Member's Bill is by no means as certain to be approved at this stage, as voting is rarely on party lines. In 1965 an alternative procedure for the second reading of Public Bills in the Commons was introduced, whereby a Minister may move that any such Bill be referred to a standing Second Reading Committee, consisting of from thirty to eighty M.P.s, which shall then report to the House, with reasons, whether or not they recommend that the Bill be read a second time. The procedure may not be used if at least twenty members rise in their places to object to the Minister's motion. But if a Bill is sent to the Second Reading Committee, the report of the Committee must be put to the House for a vote without amendment or debate. This has resulted in a saving of Parliamentary time, and the passage of many non-controversial Bills for which the Government would not otherwise have been able to find debating time.

If the Bill is defeated at its second reading it is then withdrawn, but if it is approved by a majority of the voters in the count it goes on into the committee stage. In this stage a committee of the House,[1] whose membership is allotted in the proportion that the parties have in the House, or in some cases a committee consisting of the whole House, will consider the detailed provisions or clauses, as they are called, of the Bill. In the consideration of a very long Bill time limits sometimes have to be set for this stage,[2] but usually the committee is able to discuss and alter if necessary any part of the Bill it thinks fit. At this stage the party majority of the Government is not so important, as voting is not upon the general principles of the Bill, now accepted, but merely upon how best to formulate the detailed provisions throughout the Bill. After the committee stage is over the committee reports to the whole House what it has done. At this, the report stage, it is still possible for the House to amend the Bill, but this is not often done in practice. Finally the Bill receives its third reading, when a last debate is held upon the general principles of the measure.

---

[1] Committees of the Houses sit for many purposes of which this is only one, though perhaps the most important.

[2] The "Kangaroo" (only certain amendments are chosen for debate) and the "Guillotine" (a time limit is placed on the debate of each part of a measure). These methods are not confined, however, to debate in committee.

Again it is possible for the Bill to be defeated, but if it has already passed the other stages, particularly the second reading, it is most unlikely that this will occur. As far as details are concerned it is usual that only amendments of slips in the wording of the Bill are made. Once it has passed the third reading it has "passed the House". In 1967 the House of Commons' Select Committee on Procedure made recommendations designed to cut out waste of time and repetition of debate in the report stage and third reading of Public Bills, and it seems possible that the House may soon authorise some report stages to be concluded in committee, and place restrictions upon the power of members to move amendments in a third reading.

Having been approved in one House, the Bill must now go to the other House and pass through similar stages in the course of the same session of Parliament. If the Bill should be approved in the second House in the same form in which it eventually passed the first House, then it will be sent forthwith for the Royal Assent, and will become an Act of Parliament. If on the other hand it is approved in principle, but altered in some respect in its details, then it will be returned for further consideration in the first House. If the amendments of the second chamber are then agreed to in the first chamber the Bill will go for the Royal Assent, but if no such agreement can be reached after a reasonable time the Bill was, up till 1911, treated as defeated, just as if the second House had rejected the Bill outright. The Parliament Acts of 1911 and 1949 have, however, altered this position greatly, and the effect of these Acts will be considered after the procedure for other types of Bill has been discussed.

B. *Private Bills*

Private Bills are either local or personal. Local Private Bills for the most part concern some particular locality in the country, and are usually initiated by local authorities, whereas personal Private Bills deal with the affairs of certain particular persons or estates. Not all personal Bills, however, are necessarily Private Bills, and, for example, personal Indemnity Bills are usually Public Bills. Local Bills may be considered first in either House, but personal Private Bills must go through the Lords before the Commons. In each House the stages of the Bill are for the most part similar to those employed in the case of Public Bills, but a major difference appears in committee, for at that stage any interested party at all may appear and oppose the Bill, and witnesses may be called, so that the procedure takes on a quasi-judicial aspect. In addition the members of the committee who conduct this inquiry must be entirely disinterested in the affairs concerned in the Bill. This procedure is the outcome of a desire to protect the interests of those affected parties whose causes would not be likely to excite public interest. Once a Private Bill has passed one House it is unlikely to be altered or opposed in the other, though this does occasionally occur. After passing both Houses, the Bill goes for the Royal Assent.

C. *Hybrid Bills*

When a Hybrid Bill is under consideration the opportunity for interested parties to appear at the committee stage must be given, but otherwise the procedure adopted is similar to that where a Public Bill is under consideration. Thus the members of the committee need not be disinterested.

In the case of all Bills the Royal Assent is required before they become law. Sometimes a Norman-French formula is used to signify the assent, though it is not customary now for the Monarch to assent in person. But the assent is usually just notified to each House by the Speaker of the Commons and the Lord Chancellor respectively, under the powers provided in the Royal Assent Act, 1967.

The Parliament Acts, 1911 *and* 1949

From the foregoing account it will be seen that originally it was possible for either House to veto the legislative endeavours of the other by refusing to pass Bills sent to it from the other. Convention had it that the non-representative chamber, the Lords, should not so obstruct the Commons if the Commons had become set upon the passage of a particular measure, but nevertheless the Lords broke this convention several times during 1908 and 1909, when the Commons had a huge Liberal Party majority. After two general elections and considerable political rancour and bitterness, the Government prevailed upon the Lords to allow a Parliament Bill to pass the upper chamber, by holding over it the promise of the King that he would if necessary create a sufficient number of new peers who would support its passage. The provisions of the resulting Parliament Act, 1911, were altered even further to the detriment of the power of the Lords by the Parliament Act, 1949, which was passed under the procedure laid down in the Act of 1911. The procedure provided for in the two Acts is as follows:

(1) In the case of a *Money Bill* having passed the Commons, it shall receive the Royal Assent without the approval of the Lords unless it has been passed by the Lords within one month of being sent to the Lords, provided that the Bill was sent to the Lords at least one month before the end of the session. This, therefore, strengthens the previous constitutional convention that financial Bills should only begin in the Commons, and should not be altered by the Lords. The Acts provide guidance for the Speaker of the Commons as to what Bills are properly to be regarded as Money Bills, but the Speaker is nevertheless legally empowered to certify any Bill as a Money Bill in theory, for the Acts provide that the Speaker's certificate to this effect is final and cannot be questioned in any court of law.

(2) The power of the Lords to reject any Bill attempting to extend the maximum duration of Parliament beyond five years is left unimpaired.

(3) In the case of any other *Public Bill* the power of the Lords to obstruct the wishes of the Commons by rejection, complete or partial, has been severely curtailed. Under the provisions of the Acts, if a Bill has been passed in the Commons and then rejected in the Lords, and in the next session of Parliament it is again passed by the Commons, but the House of Lords does not also pass it without amendments (except amendments approved by the Commons), then the Commons is empowered to send it up for the Royal Assent despite the Lords' opposition. It is also provided that at least one year must have elapsed between the second reading of the Bill in the Commons in the first session and the third reading in the Commons in the second session. When this procedure has been adopted because of the Lords' opposition to a Public Bill, the Speaker of the House of Commons must endorse the Bill with a certificate that it has been passed by the Commons according to the procedure laid down in the Parliament Acts before it is sent up for the Royal Assent. Again this certificate is final.

It will be noted that the Acts do not deal with Private Bills, and therefore the power of the Lords to veto Private Bills if the House should so wish is left untouched. The Lords no longer has any practical power over Money Bills at all, and theoretically it would be possible for the Speaker to certify any Bill as a Money Bill, though an abuse of this authority would very probably have disastrous political repercussions. It is in any case most unlikely in the British Parliamentary system that the Prime Minister would be able to persuade the Speaker to take such a step. The delaying power of the Lords over other Public Bills, with the one exception of Bills to extend the life of Parliament, is now just one year. Under the Act of 1911 it was two years, and this cutting down of the time was the *raison d'être* of the 1949 Act. The Parliament Acts make clear the Commons' control over public finances, and they assert the supremacy of the Commons over the Lords, though of course it would always be open to any Parliament to alter the position by future legislation. This is, however, most unlikely to occur so long as the Lords remains basically an hereditary chamber. One of the reasons why the parties have found it so difficult to formulate an agreement on the basis of which to reform the composition of the Lords has been that such agreed reform might have to carry with it an increase in the actual power of the second chamber. This largely explains the general opposition of the Labour Party to most schemes so far suggested. Although there is at present a permanent Conservative majority in the Lords, the Labour Party has been reasonably content with this state of affairs because it is a largely powerless majority in any case of real conflict. The Parliament (No. 2) Bill had to be abandoned in 1969 partly because so many M.P.s could see the impracticability of the clauses in it designed to reduce still further the Lords' power to delay legislation. Yet any reformed and re-invigorated House might be less helpless against the wishes of a resolute Commons.

It is, however, fair to add that the House of Lords has rarely been obstructive during the past fifty years, and that the Lords' amendments to Bills are more often accepted by the Commons than rejected. The peers only rarely vote on strict party lines, and it may be asserted that the passage of the Parliament Acts in a sense proved to be the saviour of the upper House. Once it is clear that their will cannot prevail over the Commons, the efforts of peers in the discharge of their Parliamentary functions have naturally become more consistently constructive. It is suggested that the House of Lords now exercises much more use-fully than in former times those functions which the members of the famous Conference of 1917–1918, presided over by Lord Bryce, considered ought to be discharged by the second chamber. These functions are the examination and revision of Bills first dealt with in the Commons, the delaying of Bills for so long, and no longer, as may be needed to enable national opinion to be expressed upon them, the initiation of less controversial Bills which can be expected to pass through the Commons fairly easily, and the full and free discussion of important matters for which the Commons may not immediately be able to find time. A recent authority has asserted that the House of Lords is the best second chamber in the Commonwealth, and one which stands comparison with its counterparts in almost any developed country.[1]

IV. Other Functions of Parliament

It would be a great mistake to think of Parliament only as a legislative assembly. In fact legislative business occupies only about one-half of the time taken by the sittings of Parliament. Nevertheless it is the legislative business and power of Parliament which is of importance to lawyers, who are only concerned to discover and to apply law; and it is only when legislating that Parliament is responsible for the creation of law, as the term legislation itself would imply. It is therefore not necessary to elaborate here upon the other functions of Parliament, but, in order to aid a full understanding of Parliament, which is a deliberative as well as a legislative assembly, the most important of them at the present day will be listed:

(1) General debate, which may take place in either House upon any subject it deems fit to examine. There is no necessity for there to be any vote upon a motion, but often such a vote does take place, and frequently along party lines. Some of the subjects chosen for debate are put forward by the Government, and others by the Opposition, for the time of Parliament is allotted by the Leaders of each House partly to matters the Government wishes discussed and partly to subjects chosen by the Opposition. Here, as in the second and third functions mentioned

---

[1] S. A. de Smith, *Constitutional and Administrative Law* (2nd ed., 1973), p. 297.

below, it can be seen that Parliament, or at least the House of Commons, acts as a bridge between the people and the Government, through the agency of the people's elected representatives.

(2) Questions may be addressed by any member, usually to a Minister, upon any subject connected with the administration or public affairs for which the Minister or member is officially responsible, providing that it does not concern proceedings pending in Parliament. Often the questions are suggested by constituents. It is obvious that unless a proper answer of a more or less satisfactory nature is made the subject is likely to give rise to some agitation. It may be noted here that one of the salient differences between the procedure of the United Kingdom Parliament and that of the United States Congress is that there is no "question time" in the latter, largely because members of the Government do not sit in Congress.

(3) The making of Ministerial statements, which may or may not be followed by debate.

(4) Work in committees. This is often upon Bills, as has been seen above, but it may be upon matters of any kind referred for inquiry to a committee by the House. The Public Accounts Committee and the Select Committees on Estimates and on the Nationalised Industries play an important part in keeping a check on the administrative process. In recent years Parliament has experimented with the introduction of other committees to investigate broad fields of administrative activity. Occasionally joint committees of the two Houses sit for the purpose of discussing matters of common concern, and in particular there is a joint committee to consider all Bills covering statute law revision and the consolidation of previous enactments.

(5) The consideration of the privileges of the two Houses, which will be discussed more fully below.

(6) The House of Lords, but not the Commons, is also the highest court of appeal for England, Northern Ireland and, in civil cases only, for Scotland. This topic will be discussed in Chapter 4.

V. PARLIAMENTARY PRIVILEGE

In order that members of both Houses may carry out their tasks without undue interference or fear, certain privileges have

attached to them since very early times. The historical reason
for their existence is that Parliament is strictly the "High Court
of Parliament", and superior courts of law maintain similar
privileges which protect them in the exercise of their judicial
functions. Although they are mainly similar in each House, for
the privileges belong essentially to Parliament as a whole, there are
some differences in effect. The privileges common to members
of both Houses are:

(1) Freedom of speech in debate from any outside interference
at all. This privilege has been undoubted since the ultimate
triumph of Parliament over Stuart despotism in the seventeenth
century. The meaning of "debate" appears to have been
widened considerably, for this privilege covers also communica-
tions between members or made to members by their constituents upon Parliamentary business. Such missives would therefore
be immune from any operation of the law of libel, as they are
considered by the House to be "proceedings in Parliament". A
recent limitation upon the meaning of this phrase and upon this
privilege which has been imposed by the House of Commons
itself will be discussed below.

(2) Freedom from arrest during sessions of Parliament and for
forty days before or after a session. A peer, however, remains
permanently covered by this privilege. But it is not as wide as
it may seem, for it probably only covers civil arrest, now
practically unknown. It is still debatable whether a member
of either House is privileged from arrest for summary offences,
though the absence of authority upon the point shows its
comparative practical unimportance. A Select Committee on
Parliamentary Privilege recommended, in 1967, the abolition
by statute of freedom from arrest so far as members of the
House of Commons are concerned.

(3) The Commons have the right of access to the Monarch
through the Speaker, whereas each peer has theoretically the
right of individual access, probably very rarely exercised.

(4) Each House has the right to regulate the qualifications for
its membership, subject to any statute which may have been
passed on the subject, and to regulate its own internal

proceedings. Thus, much of the foregoing account of procedure in the passing of Bills is a matter upon which the courts cannot inquire.

(5) The right to impeach, that is, to try any person for any offence in the House of Lords, with the Commons acting as prosecutors. This appears now to be obsolete, not having been exercised for over 150 years, and its abolition was in any case recommended by the Select Committee in 1967.

(6) The right of each House to punish for breach of privilege or contempt of the House. The privileges are those listed in this chapter, but contempt may in theory be anything which offends the dignity of the House. Whether anything amounts to a contempt or a breach of privilege is for the House itself to decide, and the courts have no cognisance of such a problem, except in the one instance where either House punishes a person, as for example by imprisonment, for a breach of privilege, but gives a patently bad reason for doing so. On a subsequent application for habeas corpus[1] the court may declare the proceeding to be unlawful,[2] but if no reason for the claim of the House should be given it would be impossible for any court to interfere.[3] Punishment awarded by the House may be by

---

[1] See Chapter 8, *post*.
[2] See *e.g. Stockdale* v. *Hansard* (1839), 9 Ad. & El.1. There a report of prison commissioners contained a libel of Stockdale, and the Commons had ordered the Parliamentary printers, Messrs. Hansard, to publish the report for sale to the public. In the subsequent libel action by Stockdale, Hansard, under instructions from the Commons, pleaded that the report had been published by order of the House, and that it was therefore covered by Parliamentary privilege. The court held that this was not one of the privileges of the House. Freedom of speech covered papers passed between members themselves, but not those allowed to pass into the hands of the general public.
[3] As occurred in the *Case of the Sheriff of Middlesex* (1840), 11 Ad. & El.273, which was the sequel to *Stockdale* v. *Hansard, supra*. The Commons had passed a resolution that the publication of reports etc. was essential for the proper functioning of Parliament, and that the House had the sole right of judging the validity and extent of any privileges claimed. The House allowed the damages to be paid in Stockdale's case, but made it clear that any future attempt to bring such an action would itself amount to a contempt of the House. Nevertheless Stockdale proceeded to bring another similar action against Hansard, and judgment was given in Stockdale's favour in the absence of any plea by the defendant, but when the Sheriff of Middlesex levied the damages awarded in this latter case, and he refused to give the sum back when so ordered by the Commons, he was forthwith imprisoned by order of the Commons for contempt and breach of privilege of the House. Although the Sheriff applied for habeas corpus, his application failed because the Speaker's warrant of committal did not contain any reason for the allegation of contempt or breach of privilege.

imprisonment, fine (probably this is only possible in the Lords), reprimand, admonition or, in the case of a member of the House, expulsion. The most common recent instances of this privilege being exercised are concerned with contempt by journalists, and with disorderly behaviour in the House.

In addition to the above each House has certain other privileges. The Commons maintains the right to control finance and initiate financial legislation. Originally this was mere convention, but the existence of the privilege has been strengthened by statute in the Parliament Acts, 1911 and 1949, as described above. The Commons also claims as a privilege that the Crown will place the best construction on its deliberations, a privilege now of no practical importance. The additional privileges of the Lords are more numerous, but of very little real importance. They include the right to summon judges for advice on questions of law (in practice now never exercised, because of the presence in the House of the Lords of Appeal in Ordinary since the Appellate Jurisdiction Act, 1876)[1], exemption from jury service, and the right of any peer alone to enter a protest against any measure of the House in its Journals.

A final word on the subject of Parliamentary privilege as a living issue should be said. The original reason for the existence of the privileges, that is to protect the *High Court* of Parliament, has practically disappeared, for, except where the House of Lords acts as a final court of appeal, the real functions of Parliament are now those of debate and legislation. It cannot any longer be the case that all the existing privileges are necessary to protect members in the discharge of their duties. In particular it may be argued that the power to punish should be transferred from the Houses themselves to the courts of law, so that the Houses may no longer seem to be judges in their own cause. Indeed it is possible that only the safeguarding of freedom of speech actually inside Parliament is now necessary to ensure the existence of a

---

Ultimately the Parliamentary Papers Act was passed in 1840 to make law the very extension of privilege which the Commons had claimed, and the Sheriff was set free when the session of Parliament ended shortly afterwards. The enactment of the statute may perhaps be regarded as an act of conscience by the Commons.

[1] The judges were last summoned in an English appeal in *Allen* v. *Flood*, [1898] A.C. 1, [1895-9] All E.R. Rep. 52, and in a Scottish appeal in *Free Church of Scotland (General Assembly)* v. *Lord Overtoun*, [1904] A.C. 515.

free and virile assembly. In the present state of the law, however, it is to be expected that members will not claim privilege frivolously or unless there is real need to do so. The record of the House of Lords in this respect has in modern times been good, and it is extremely rare today for any peer to claim privilege. On the other hand the Commons has in the present century acquired a certain notoriety for its eagerness to claim and assert privilege. A standing committee of the House, the Committee of Privileges, meets quite frequently to consider alleged cases referred to it and to advise the whole House upon its proper course of action. Divers activities of individuals outside the House may be held by the House to amount to contempt,[1] and the courts of law are powerless to decide otherwise.[2] Often the cases alleged are not really infringements of the necessary freedom of the House, but merely instances where M.P.s have felt annoyed about things said of them.[3] Public feeling has on occasions been roused by what one may well consider abuse of the essential privileges of the House. It is a subject which has been much canvassed in letters to newspapers— the writers themselves having been in danger of the wrath of the Commons! But the general public and the courts can work no changes or diminution in the power of the House. It is therefore for the House itself to use these powers with discretion and good sense; the virtue of the preservation of freedom should not be permitted to turn into the vice of tyranny. It is encouraging that on July 8th, 1958,[4] the House decided by a small majority that a letter written by a member to a Minister was not necessarily a "proceeding in Parliament", thus rendering the writer immune from the law of defamation. Mr. George Strauss, M.P., had written a letter to the Paymaster-General, who represented the Minister of Power (a peer) in the Commons. In it he alleged that the London Electricity Board had behaved in a scandalous manner in the way in which it invited tenders for the purchase of its scrap metal. The contents of the letter were disclosed to the Board, which,

---

[1] *E.g. R. v. Paty* (1704), 2 Ld. Raym.1105, where five Aylesbury men had brought an action against the returning officers for refusing their votes at an election. They were committed to prison by order of the Commons for breach of privilege.
[2] *E.g. Case of the Sheriff of Middlesex* (see note 3, p. 24, *ante*).
[3] *E.g.* the offence taken by M.P.s at the comments in the *Sunday Express* upon the methods of allocating petrol ration coupons: 563 H.C.Deb.407 (1957).
[4] 591 H.C.Deb.208.

after some exchange of correspondence, informed Mr. Strauss that it intended to sue him for libel. Although Mr. Strauss claimed that this was a breach of the privileges of the House, a claim which was supported by the Report to the House of the Committee of Privileges, this claim was rejected on a free vote in the House. The status of such letters in the future will depend upon their actual nature, and their writers will only be absolutely privileged where the contents can be truly considered to pertain to Parliamentary business, or the duty of the writer as a member of one of the Houses of Parliament. It is perhaps worth noting that, as a result of a subsequent official inquiry into the activities of the London Electricity Board, it was found that no such irregularities as had been alleged in Mr. Strauss's letter had in fact taken place. The present indications are that M.P.s since the Strauss affair have been more circumspect about claiming that their privileges have been infringed[1], and in 1967 the Select Committee on Parliamentary Privilege set up by the Commons recommended a number of changes in procedure to reduce the publicity attendant upon complaints of breach of privilege, and to cause the House to use its penal jurisdiction more sparingly. In order to get rid of the false impression of members of the Commons as a "privileged class", the Committee further suggested that the term "privilege" should be replaced by that of "rights and immunities." But this Report has yet to be implemented.

VI. THE SOVEREIGNTY OF PARLIAMENT

It is common to say that Parliament may do anything it wishes, that it is supreme. In law this is true, and it is perhaps the most fundamental rule of British constitutional law. The only limitation is not a legal one but that of political expediency.[2] Yet Parliamentary supremacy only concerns the legislative Acts of Parliament. Only these must be obeyed by courts of law, and no mere resolution or debate or answer to a question is of any importance as far

---

[1] See D. C. M. Yardley, "The House of Commons and its Privileges since the Strauss Affair", (1962) XV *Parliamentary Affairs* 500.

[2] For a stimulating account of this principle see H. W. R. Wade, "The Basis of Legal Sovereignty" [1955] *Cambridge Law Journal* 1972. See, however, the reference to the European Convention on Human Rights, *post*, p. 35.

as the law is concerned.[1] Statute law, therefore, is all-powerful, for it may do anything Parliament wishes; in this sense Parliament is the sovereign body in the land, provided it conforms to the necessary procedure of legislation.

In Anglo-Saxon and Norman times this was not the position. The Monarch, as a result of political and factual autonomy, sometimes brought about by conquest, was supreme. He was lord of all land and dispensed all laws. When Parliament was first convened in the course of the middle ages it was with his leave, even though in fact it is possible that he might have found it politically unwise to deny its members the right so to meet. But once Parliament was established as an institution it gradually gained in power and jurisdiction, until in the seventeenth century it became necessary for it to indulge in a trial of strength with the Monarchy. It is not within our present purpose to trace in any detail the fluctuations of that struggle, which at its extreme pitch led to the Civil War in the 1640s and the Bloodless Revolution of 1688–1689, but suffice it to say that by the time of that latter event Parliament was triumphant and the Monarch was forced to acknowledge its supremacy. It may well be submitted that what had taken place was in fact a political revolution, and that in law nothing could wrest the power of the Monarch from him but his own voluntary surrender. This may be so, and the Stuart Kings were not prepared to make such a surrender, but Parliament found the ultimate solution in 1688 by getting rid of the reigning Monarch, James II, assuming supreme power, and inviting two new Monarchs, William III and Mary II, to occupy the throne jointly, providing they agreed to acknowledge the supremacy of Parliament. In this way the positions were reversed, and the new Monarchs reigned by leave of Parliament. In theory there are still a large number of Royal Prerogatives which may be exercised without recourse to the consent of Parliament, and these will be examined in the next chapter, but there is no doubt that any Parliament has the power, if it should so wish, to alter or abolish any such Prerogatives which it finds uncongenial, providing such alteration or abolition is carried out by an Act of Parliament and in no other way.

---

[1] See *e.g.* the stand taken by the Court of Queen's Bench in *Stockdale* v. *Hansard*, cited in note 2, p. 24, *ante*.

The most important instrument which gave evidence of this newly won sovereignty of Parliament was the Bill of Rights, 1689. In origin this was not in fact a statute at all, for it was drawn up at a time when James II had fled the country and no Monarch reigned, but William and Mary had to agree to its provisions before Parliament would allow them to assume the throne. As a matter of historical fact, Parliament and William reached an amicable agreement, but there is no doubt that Parliament held the whip hand in the negotiations, for it had a throne to give away, but only on its own terms. In particular the Bill of Rights destroyed the power of any Monarch to suspend the operation of a law, or to dispense with it in any individual instance, save where such dispensation had not been "assumed and exercised of late", a loophole by which the Prerogative right of pardon was preserved. Again the sole power to levy taxation was finally vested in Parliament, after what had been a long-drawn out struggle, thus re-embodying and expanding the principle that taxation requires the *consent* of the tax-payers (as now represented by Parliament), which was originally included in Magna Carta, 1215.[1] It is this control of the national purse-strings which has made Parliament's position so secure today.

It may be possible to say that the ultimate real power in any nation rests in its people, who, at least in theory, control their representatives. We might say that a new nation arose in 1689, vesting its greatest power in Parliament, and that a political revolution occurred in 1688–1689, just as it had occurred in 1066 and several times in Lancastrian and Yorkist times, when the identity of the Monarch was changed after resort to force. Whatever the cause, from the new order stemmed the new law. Thus our modern constitutional system and law dates from 1689. This we must accept, but the Jacobites would have been the rightful claimants to the throne if it had not been for the Revolution.

Since Parliament from that time has possessed supreme power, it follows naturally that it should be able to retain this power. It

---

[1] Magna Carta was not in fact a statute in the sense that is meant today, for it merely set out the demands of the barons to which King John was forced to assent at Runnymede. Nevertheless it has always been treated as having the force and authority of a statute, both by the courts and by Parliament. It therefore must come within the confines of that fundamental law of the land which it is our purpose to discuss in this book.

is for this reason that Parliament is said not to be able to bind its successors. Although Parliament may pass a statute in, say, 1974, by which it can enact some completely new law, yet it is still within the power of Parliament ten years later, or even only six months later, to abolish or alter that law in any way it thinks fit by a later statute, and such alteration, amendment or abolition may even take place by implication from the later enactment, if it is inconsistent with the former.[1] Perhaps the most striking example of Parliament's power to repeal former enactments is provided by the Irish Free State (Constitution) Act, 1922, which severed that part of Ireland which is now the Republic of Ireland from the rest of the United Kingdom in flagrant violation of the Act of Union with Ireland, 1800, which had declared the union of the two Kingdoms of Great Britain and Ireland to be "for ever". The 1800 Act also provided for the permanent establishment of the United Church of England and Ireland, yet the Church of Ireland was disestablished by the Irish Church Act, 1869.

In 1971 Salmon, L.J., put the position graphically in a case in which a Mr. Blackburn failed to persuade the Court of Appeal to grant a declaration that the United Kingdom application to join the European Communities was illegal because it would be an "irreversible partial surrender of the Sovereignty of the Crown in Parliament". Salmon, L.J., said: "As to Parliament, in the present state of the law, it can enact, amend and repeal any legislation it pleases."[2] On the other hand, Lord Denning, M.R., in the same case put the practical realities of the issue into perspective. He said: "We have all been brought up to believe that, in legal theory, one Parliament cannot bind another and that no Act is irreversible. But legal theory does not always march alongside political reality. Take the Statute of Westminster 1931, which takes away the power of Parliament to legislate for the Dominions. Can anyone imagine that Parliament could or would reverse that Statute? Take the Acts which have granted independence to the Dominions and territories overseas. Can anyone imagine that Parliament could or would reverse these laws and take away their independence? Most clearly not. Free-

---

[1] As was held in *Vauxhall Estates, Ltd.* v. *Liverpool Corporation*, [1932] 1 K.B. 733, followed by the Court of Appeal in *Ellen Street Estates, Ltd.* v. *Minister of Health*, [1934] 1 K.B. 590; [1934] All E.R. Rep. 385.
[2] *Blackburn* v. *A.-G.*, [1971] 1 W.L.R. 1037, at 1041.

dom once given cannot be taken away. Legal theory must give
way to practical politics."[1]

At this stage it might well be asked whether the Parliament
Acts, 1911 and 1949, have the effect of binding Parliament for
the future as to its procedure in the passage of certain types of
statute. But again the answer must be in the negative, for it is
perfectly feasible that Parliament should one day abolish or amend
that legislation. Parliament may always at any time legislate for
the alteration of the procedure or composition of itself, and the
Life Peerages Act, 1958, and the Peerage Act, 1963, mentioned
above, are good illustrations of the application of this truth. It is
important, however, to remember that in each case it must act by
the composition and according to the procedure which may happen
to be legally in force at the time, otherwise it would be possible for
some impostor assembly to call itself the true Parliament of the
realm. This, after all, is why the courts will not recognise the
validity of a mere resolution of either House as law. Nevertheless
the internal procedure of each House (as opposed to the relationship between the two Houses) is outside the purview of the courts,
for it is within the privileges of the Houses, as has been pointed out
above, to declare whether or not the proper procedure applicable
in any event has been followed. As Lord Campbell once said, "All
that a Court of Justice can do is to look to the Parliament roll: if
from that it should appear that a Bill has passed both Houses and
received the Royal Assent, no Court of Justice can enquire into
the mode in which it was introduced into Parliament, nor into
what was done previous to its introduction, or what passed in
Parliament during its progress in its various stages through both
Houses".[2]

Yet the power of the courts to interpret Acts can sometimes be
used in effect to thwart the intention of Parliament, though the
courts do not overtly admit this. Thus in *Anisminic, Ltd.* v. *Foreign
Compensation Commission*[3] the House of Lords was faced with a

---

[1] *Blackburn* v. *A.-G.*, [1971] 1 W.L.R. 1037, at 1040.
[2] *Edinburgh and Dalkeith Rly.* v. *Wauchope* (1842), 8 Cl & Fin. 710. *Cf.
Pickin* v. *British Railways Board* [1972] 3 All E.R. 923; [1973] 1 Q.B. 219,
where the Court of Appeal held that it was competent to draw the attention of
Parliament to any false material included in the Preamble to a Private Bill
which had subsequently been passed. The court, by investigating whether the
Act had been properly obtained, could thus prevent undue advantage being taken
of Parliament.
[3] [1969] 1 All E.R. 208; [1969] 2 A.C. 147.

statutory provision that a decision of the Commission "shall not be called in question in any court of law." Yet the Lords held that a determination by the Commission made *ultra vires* was void, and therefore not a decision at all, so that the court was perfectly free to set it aside. Perhaps this only illustrated how the British doctrine of Parliamentary sovereignty is always dependent upon the acquiescence of the courts in it, and shows that it will only remain so long as the courts allow it to remain.

There is, in fact, a great deal of dispute among jurists as to whether Parliament, though always unfettered in area of legislative jurisdiction, may find itself bound as to the manner and form in which it may legislate. For example, would Parliament be bound by any radical change it might make in its composition, such as by abolishing the House of Lords (as was actually stated in the Preamble to the Parliament Act, 1911, to be Parliament's future intention)? Again, it is far from clear whether the undoubtedly sovereign legislature, Parliament, must always remain in its present form. Is it necessary in law for Parliament to be composed of the Monarch, the Lords and the Commons, or can the three component parts be differently named and formed, or be reduced in number, as has occurred in New Zealand? Could the Monarchy be abolished legally, and a President or Head of State put in the place of the Monarch? Or would Parliament be bound by any repeal of the Bill of Rights, 1689, and fresh subordination of itself to the Monarch? A legislative organ is of course necessary in any modern state, if chaos is to be avoided, but it is far from clear whether the British Parliament's legal power to change the law and to legislate upon constitutional matters also includes the power to abolish or change itself radically for the future. The problem will never be solved because any such change would depend for its validity upon the continued support or otherwise of the people, a political and not a legal factor; and jurists would still argue as to whether the new order came into being by law or by political revolution. The past precedents, which include the abdication of sovereignty by the Parliaments of England and Scotland in favour of the new Parliament of Great Britain in 1706, and by the Parliament of Great Britain in favour of the new Parliament of the United Kingdom in 1800, are equally unhelpful for this reason.[1]

---

[1] For further reading and the opposing views upon this problem, the following selection of materials might be studied: H. W. R. Wade, "The Basis of Legal

After a decade of negotiations the United Kingdom joined the European Community on 1st January, 1973, as a result of the European Communities Act, 1972, implementing the Treaty of Accession signed in 1971. The Community in fact consists of three Communities in number, the European Coal and Steel Community (E.C.S.C.), the European Economic Community (E.E.C.), and the European Atomic Energy Community (Euratom), but they share the same institutions. These are the European Parliament, consisting at present of members of the national Parliaments, nominated by those Parliaments; the Council of Ministers, consisting of one member of the Government of each member state; and the Commission, consisting of thirteen leading personalities, who must be nationals of member states, although not more than two members may have the same nationality, and all of whom are chosen for their "general competence and indisputable independence." The European Parliament has no real legislative power, though it must be consulted on all important acts of the Community, and the Commission, which is the executive organ of the Community, is responsible to it and may be compelled to resign by a vote of censure. The Parliament has no similar control, however, over the Council of Ministers, which is the essential decision-making body of the Community, assisted in all its work by the Commission. According to Community law, therefore, national Parliaments and their representatives in the European Parliament lose their control over matters entrusted by the Treaty to the Council. The Commission, in its function as executive organ, may make *recommendations* to member states, which are not of binding obligation, but it may also make *decisions*, which are binding upon named addressees, *directives*, which are binding in substance but leave to each member state its choice as to how to enforce them, and *regulations* which, subject to prior approval by the Council, are directly applicable in each member state.

Sovereignty", [1955] *Cambridge Law Journal* 172; H. R. Gray, "The Sovereignty of Parliament Today", (1953-1954) 10 *University of Toronto Law Journal* 54; T. B. Smith, *Studies Critical and Comparative* (1962), p. 1; R. F. V. Heuston, *Essays in Constitutional Law* (2nd ed., 1964), Chapter 1; G. Marshall, *Parliamentary Sovereignty and the Commonwealth* (1957), Part III and Appendices I-III; A. V. Dicey, *Introduction to the Study of the Law of the Constitution* (10th ed., by E. C. S. Wade), Introduction and Part 1; Sir W. Ivor Jennings, *The Law and the Constitution* (5th ed., 1959), Chapter IV; Sir D. L. Keir and F. H. Lawson, *Cases in Constitutional Law* (5th Ed., 1967), Part 1.

Although the major purpose of the Community is economic, it is clear that the powers of the Community organs not only render it necessary in fact for United Kingdom law to conform in some respects with the laws of its new European partners, but also make it likely that a certain amount of law will become directly applicable in the United Kingdom from time to time without having been through the normal legislative process in the United Kingdom Parliament. The Westminster Parliament is in the process of establishing a committee machinery to examine Community laws, and to see where United Kingdom law needs amendment, and a Joint Committee of both Houses of Parliament has already recommended that scrutiny of regulations made by the European Commission should be exercised by a similar Joint Committee. Does this mean that our Parliament has surrendered some portion of its sovereignty in favour of the Community institutions? Of course Parliament will undoubtedly usually want to do its best to conform with Community legislation, but successive Lord Chancellors have stated that it would remain within the power of Parliament to repeal by a subsequent Act any former Act applying a treaty which had been made. Despite some speculation to the contrary,[1] it is submitted that amendment or repeal of former legislation by implication, as mentioned above, would also continue to be possible, though the courts would probably lean as far as possible against this course in all cases of doubt. A specific Act passed later by the United Kingdom Parliament which is directly in conflict with Community legislation would, it is submitted, have to be followed by British courts. Sorting out the result of such a clash would seem to be a political, rather than legal, matter for the Government, and it may well result in later amending United Kingdom legislation. So far as basic constitutional law is concerned, therefore, entry to the European Community, though envisaged as the first stage in a process of possible European political integration, is in itself not so fundamental a change as it seems at first sight.

In 1966 the United Kingdom Government accepted the com-

---

[1] F. M. Auburn, "Trends in Comparative Constitutional Law" (1972), 35 *Modern Law Review* 129; D. G. T. Williams, "The Constitution of the United Kingdom," [1972B] *Cambridge Law Journal* 266; *cf.* F. A. Trindade, "Parliamentary Sovereignty and the Primacy of European Community Law " (1972), 35 *Modern Law Review* 375; O. Hood Phillips, *Constitutional and Administrative Law* (5th ed., 1973), pp. 75-76.

petence of the European Commission of Human Rights, as laid down by the European Convention on Human Rights, signed in 1950. This enables the legality of a United Kingdom Act of Parliament to be challenged before the Commission by any private individual. There is thus now the possibility of some external, though not internal, judicial review of United Kingdom Acts.

A final word should be said about the status of Parliamentary sovereignty in Scotland, for although it is beyond question for England, Wales and Northern Ireland, it has been doubted in a case in Scotland so far as that country is concerned. In that case, *MacCormick* v. *Lord Advocate*,[1] the use by Queen Elizabeth of the numeral "II" was disputed, primarily for the very common-sense reason that although Elizabeth I had been Queen of England she had never been Queen of Scotland, and that there had never before been a Queen of Scotland known by that name. The use of the numeral had been authorised by the Royal Titles Act, 1953, for that statute allowed Queen Elizabeth to use whatever numeral she thought fit in the United Kingdom. But it was alleged that the Treaty of Union between England and Scotland declared that any law inconsistent with such of its terms as were declared in the Treaty itself (and the subsequent Acts of the Parliaments of England and Scotland) to be unalterable was void, and therefore that it forbade the use of the numeral in this way. It was ultimately held by the Court of Session in Edinburgh that the Treaty did not actually forbid the use of the numeral, and that the petitioner had in any case no legal title or interest to sue, but there were nevertheless *dicta* to the effect that had the 1953 Act been repugnant to the Treaty, then the later Act would have been void unless it was generally approved in Scotland. It is far from clear in these *dicta* whether the sovereign body for Scotland is really the whole people (presumably expressing their will by a plebiscite, which has never before been held there), or whether it is the International Court at the Hague (though this latter suggestion is most unlikely to be correct, in view of the status of the United Kingdom as a *union*). It is not suggested that the Treaty is so fundamental as to be totally unchangeable, for statutory alterations have been made before,[2] but on those occasions the changes have never

---

[1] 1953 S.C. 396.
[2] *E.g.* by the Universities (Scotland) Act, 1853, which enacted that professors at Scottish universities need no longer be members of the Presbyterian Church of Scotland.

been challenged in the courts, and apparently must possess the approbation of the people. The solution to this puzzle is still unknown, though an application to the European Commission of Human Rights would now seem feasible, but Professor de Smith is sceptical as to the validity of the special Scots law rule today.[1] At any rate with this possible exception for Scotland[2], the principle of Parliamentary sovereignty in the United Kingdom remains one of the most basic tenets of our constitutional law.

FURTHER READING

Sir William R. Anson, *The Law and Custom of the Constitution*, Vol. I: Parliament (5th ed., by M. L. Gwyer, 1922).

Sir Thomas Erskine May, *The Law, Privileges, Proceedings and Usages of Parliament* (18th ed., by Sir Barnett Cocks, 1971).

Sir W. Ivor Jennings, *Parliament* (3rd ed., 1969).

Sir Gilbert Campion, *An Introduction to the Procedure of the House of Commons* (1947).

G. Marshall, *Parliamentary Sovereignty and the Commonwealth* (1957).

T. B. Smith, "The Union of 1707 as Fundamental Law", [1957] *Public Law* 99, reproduced in *Studies Critical and Comparative* (1962), p. 1.

A. H. Hanson and H. V. Wiseman, " The Use of Committees by the House of Commons", [1959] *Public Law*. 277.

Kilmuir, Rt. Hon. the Viscount, *The Law of Parliamentary Privilege* (pamphlet) (1959).

R. J. Barnes, *Central Government in Britain* (2nd ed., 1969).

P. S. R. F. Mathijsen, *A Guide to European Community Law* (1972).

D. Lasok and J. W. Bridge, *An Introduction to the Law and Institutions of the European Community* (1973).

---

[1] *Constitutional amd Administrative Law* (2nd ed., 1973), p. 74.

[2] One further possible, though doubtful, exception is provided by section 4 of the Statute of Westminster, 1931. For this, see Chapter 13, *post*.

CHAPTER 3

THE EXECUTIVE

The executive is the organ of state which is responsible for carrying out the law and performing the routine administration of the country. Up till the seventeenth century, as has been pointed out above in Chapter 2, the authority for this exercise of power derived from its own strength and ability to coerce opposition, but since that time it has exercised its powers with the authority of Parliament. Traditionally the Monarch is the all-powerful part of the executive, but from earliest times he has acted with advisers, and since the subordination of the executive power to that of Parliament these advisers have become so much more important that in fact they are now the active members of the executive, while the Monarch is usually only informed of decisions made and actions carried out or to be carried out. An example of this principle in practice is the custom of the Chancellor of the Exchequer to inform the Monarch of his Budget proposals each year on the day before he is due to introduce them into the House of Commons. But the executive is still in law referred to as "the Crown", and this has become a collective term to cover not merely the Monarch but the whole body of his advisers and their servants. The Crown thus symbolises the Central Government. It is correct to classify the Prime Minister as a part of the Crown, and just as correct so to place the most junior of inland revenue officials and all members of the armed forces.

For convenience the component parts of the Crown or executive may be stated to be:

(1) the Monarch,

(2) his Ministers,

(3) the Central Government Departments, staffed by the civil service, and

(4) the armed forces.

Cutting across this division, as far as (1), (2) and (3) above are concerned, is the Privy Council, which is also part of the Crown. Its nature will be explained in due course in this chapter.

I. THE MONARCH

The Monarch is the King or Queen Regnant for the time being, and holds the position of Head of State. Throughout this book the term "Monarch" is used to describe the person of the Head of State in the United Kingdom, for it is thought to be more definitive than "King" or "Queen", which may appear to refer to a particular Monarch, or "Sovereign", which may be confused with Parliamentary sovereignty. Succession to the Monarchy is hereditary under the terms of the Act of Settlement, 1701, as amended by the Act of Union with Scotland, 1707, the Act of Union with Ireland, 1800, and His Majesty's Declaration of Abdication Act, 1936. Under these statutes the heirs of Sophia, Electress of Hanover, who was a granddaughter of King James I, were to succeed to the throne according to rules similar in most respects to those governing feudal descent of land, provided that no heir may succeed to the throne unless he or she is in communion with the Church of England. The present Monarch is Queen Elizabeth II. Provision is made by the Regency Acts, 1937–1953, for the appointment of a Regent if the Monarch should be below the age of eighteen years or seriously ill, and for Counsellors of State if the Monarch should be absent from the realm.

II. THE MINISTERS OF THE CROWN

The Monarch's advisers are often collectively termed "the Government", though this phrase is misleading, for in theory the whole of the Crown is the Government. They are, however, the most vital members of the Government, for they are responsible for the formulation of executive policy. As the Crown carries out its functions under the control of Parliament, it has become a convention of the Constitution that the Ministers should be drawn from the political party with a majority in the House of Commons, or occasionally from any coalition of parties which hold such a majority. The continuation in power of any particular Government depends upon the continued support of Parliament, or, more particularly, of the Commons, and thus the legislature and the executive are closely dovetailed in the British Constitution. The Monarch has the right to choose his Prime Minister, who will in turn choose the other Ministers with the approval of the Monarch. This right of the Monarch is, however, of little real importance, as the continuation in office of the Ministers will depend upon the support of a majority in the Commons which is unlikely to be forthcoming unless they are acceptable to such a majority. The stated practice of the Labour Party is to elect a leader who alone would be supported by the party as Prime Minister, and in 1964 the Conservative Party adopted a somewhat similar practice.

The Prime Minister, with the consent of the Monarch, usually appoints to ministerial office members of either House of Parliament. Most of the Ministers will be members of the Commons,[1] and the rest by convention sit in the Lords. In the rare case of the Prime Minister appointing as Minister someone who does not sit in either House it is usual for that person to be created a peer. It is customary that the heads of the more important Ministries should be members of the Commons, so that they may explain or defend themselves and their policies in the House where the elected representatives of the people are assembled. It now appears to be a convention for the Prime Minister himself to be a member of the Commons, rather than of the Lords[2], and the Chancellor of the Exchequer must perforce sit in the lower House, which alone is concerned with financial affairs. It is not our present purpose to provide a detailed list of the Ministers, for such a list would contain the names of about 100 different offices. A few examples of those at present in existence should suffice. Among the more important offices are those of Lord Chancellor, Chancellor of the Exchequer, Secretary of State for Foreign and Commonwealth Affairs, and Home Secretary. All such Ministers are the heads of different Government Departments, which in the case of the offices just quoted are respectively the Lord Chancellor's Department, the Exchequer, the Foreign and Commonwealth Office and the Home Office. Among lesser Ministers are, *e.g.*, the Minister of Transport, the Attorney-General, Ministers of State in various

---

[1] The Ministers of the Crown Act, 1964 limits the number of Ministers who may sit in the Commons to ninety-one.

[2] Most writers assert that this practice has the status of a convention, as the last Prime Minister who sat in the Lords was Lord Salisbury (1895–1902). It may be noted that the Earl of Home was appointed Prime Minister in 1963 while a member of the Lords, and he did nor renounce his peerage under the Peerage Act, 1963 until four days later. He was then a member of neither House of Parliament for some two weeks until he had successfully fought a bye-election for a seat in the Commons.

Departments (who may be regarded roughly as second Ministers in such Departments), Parliamentary Secretaries and Under-Secretaries of State. Although all such officials are members of the Government, a small inner group of the more important Ministers is called the Cabinet, which meets frequently under the chairmanship of the Prime Minister or, if he is absent, a deputy appointed by him, and very probably formulates most Government policy, only consulting junior Ministers as and when it seems appropriate or desirable. It is impossible to say with any certainty what does take place in Cabinet meetings, as they are very secret and no publication of their transactions is allowed. Again, the Government always provides a display of unanimity concerning its policies, both in Parliament and outside. Any disagreement is ironed out in private, or else, as sometimes occurs, any Minister who cannot accept the majority view will resign from office.

III. THE CENTRAL GOVERNMENT DEPARTMENTS

All the Departments of the Crown which are concerned with the government of the country are termed Central Government Departments, and each is headed either by a Minister or, in the case of non-political Departments, such as that concerned with inland revenue or with customs and excise, by a permanent head or commissioner. Although the Ministers will change whenever a Government changes, the permanent officials will not, and even in the political Departments there will always be a permanent official at the head of the permanent staff, who will see that his Minister's policy is carried out. The permanent staff are all members of the civil service, a body of permanent Crown servants recruited into the service as a career, though legally only holding office at the pleasure of the Crown.

As in the case of the different Ministers, it is not intended to detail all the Central Government Departments. The work of most will be self-evident, as in the case of, for example, the Department of Defence, the Foreign and Commonwealth Office and the Department of the Environment. Perhaps a word should be said here about the Departments of the Lord Chancellor and of the Law Officers, as these are of particular interest to lawyers. The Lord High Chancellor of Great Britain is Keeper of the Great Seal and presides over the House of Lords both as a

legislative assembly and as a final court of appeal.[1] With the help
of his Department he selects all puisne Judges of the High Court,
Circuit Judges and Recorders, who are then formally appointed
by the Crown on his advice, and he appoints and removes all
Justices of the Peace, except those in the Duchy of Lancaster
who are appointed and removed by the Chancellor of the Duchy
of Lancaster.[2] In addition he is responsible, with the aid of his
Department, and of his Law Reform Committee and the Law
Commissioners,[3] for advising on questions of law reform. The
Law Officers are the Attorney-General and Solicitor-General for
England and Wales, and the Lord Advocate and Solicitor-General
for Scotland. The English Law Officers are usually members of the
House of Commons, and the Scottish Law Officers may be. Their
responsibilities differ slightly, but in the main they represent the
Crown in civil litigation in England (including Wales) and Scotland
respectively, and they prosecute in criminal cases of great
importance or gravity, especially murder cases. They hold
positions as the head of the Bar, and thus have some authority in
questions of professional etiquette, though most questions of this
kind are dealt with by the benchers of the Inns of Court in
London[4] or by the Faculty of Advocates in Edinburgh. They
advise other Government Departments on points of law. They or
their deputies may intervene in litigation where the interests of
the public would require such a course to be taken, for they are
the representatives of the public interest where public rights are
at stake.

All Government Departments will have powers and duties
conferred upon them by Acts of Parliament, and these may in
turn be supplemented by powers acquired under the Royal
Prerogative, which will be examined later in this chapter. Although

---

[1] On this subject see Chapter 4, *post.*
[2] The nature of these various judicial offices will be explained in Chapter 4,
post.
[3] The Law Commissions Act, 1965 establishes two Commissions, one for
England and Wales, and the other for Scotland, responsible to the Lord
Chancellor, and with the duty to review the law with a view to its systematic
development and reform, including preparation for codification and the repeal
of obsolete and unnecessary Acts.
[4] A new General Council of the Inns of Court and the Bar, which will have
general powers to govern the profession and to exercise disciplinary authority,
is likely to be set up shortly.

in the past it was more usual for statutes to confer powers upon the Monarch, it is now common to find statutes conferring such duties or powers upon Ministers or Departments direct and by name. In view of the majority support in the Commons which any Government should be able to command, and which it must command in order to remain an effective Government, it may be that the Government does from time to time have a tendency to dictate to Parliament by telling it what it intends to do and relying on its party majority to carry through its proposals. Thus, although Parliament still in theory maintains the whip-hand over the executive, in practice the reverse may sometimes be more true. Where this is so the result may sometimes be regrettable, but it cannot be denied that inevitably it gives rise to strong government in a way unknown in, for example, France during the last hundred years, at least up till the establishment of the Fifth Republic in 1958, for there the multiplication of political parties led to the necessity of a succession of coalition Governments. Although there is a danger of the British Government acting in a highhanded way occasionally, yet the legal sovereignty of Parliament is always present, and no Government would be able to try the patience or conscience of its own customary supporters too far without finding an incipient rebellion on its hands.

IV. THE PRIVY COUNCIL

The Privy Council has a far longer history than the present Cabinet or Government system. It dates from Anglo-Saxon and early Norman origins, and was an earlier body of advisers of the Monarch. Although the present Cabinet has really usurped this ancient position of the Privy Council, the older body has never become entirely obsolete, and it still has some important functions. Appointment to the Council is still technically by the Monarch himself, although membership is now partly conventional and partly arranged according to the wishes of the Government of the day, with the one distinction that members are appointed for life. The conventional members are:

(a) the Lord President of the Council, who normally presides at any of the Council's meetings, and who is in any case a member of the Government for the time being;

(b) the Archbishops of Canterbury and York;

(c) the Speaker of the House of Commons;

(d) all present and former Cabinet Ministers, but not other members of the Government; and

(e) the Lords of Appeal in Ordinary, the Lords Justices of Appeal, the Lord Chief Justice, the Master of the Rolls and the President of the Probate, Divorce and Admiralty Division of the High Court.

Other persons who from time to time attain the rank of Privy Councillor, as and when the Monarch or the Government decide on such appointment, are usually leading statesmen from other Commonwealth countries, or peers or distinguished persons from any walk of life.

The purposes of the Privy Council today are several, but it only meets as a full body (about 300 Privy Councillors are usually living at any one time) on the death of the Monarch, when it will make all arrangements for the funeral, accession and coronation that may be necessary. This meeting of the Council is sometimes known as an Accession Council. Otherwise the meetings of the Privy Council are always in small bodies or as committees. The most important function is that of making Proclamations or Orders in Council. Proclamations may be made under the Royal Prerogative, to be explained in the next few pages, usually on the advice of the Prime Minister. Orders in Council are largely made under statutory powers, and will be considered more fully in Chapter 10 below. Committees of the Council sit for various purposes, such as to deal with constitutional issues concerning the Universities of Oxford and Cambridge, or the Scottish Universities, to direct research in certain fields, and to hear appeals from other countries within the Commonwealth.[1]

V. THE ARMED FORCES

All members of the Royal Navy, Army and Royal Air Force[2]

---

[1] In the Judicial Committee of the Privy Council: see Chapter 4, *post.*

[2] This is not an exclusive list, for these services are now divided up in many ways. The principles cited in this section cover all members of the regular armed forces, including, for example, the Royal Marines and the women's services. The various reserve and auxiliary forces are also included. The Home Guard, which no longer exists as an armed force, was in the same position, and doubtless would be again if ever it were reconstituted.

are servants of the Crown, and thus these services may be regarded as being parts of the Crown. The powers of the armed forces and their members are controlled partly by Acts of Parliament direct and partly through certain prerogative powers of the Crown. All members of the armed forces are dismissable by the Crown at will, and at common law no action will lie at the suit of a serviceman against the Crown for arrears of pay, or for wrongful dismissal or the refusal of a pension after service ceases[1], unless such a pension has been fixed by statute.

VI. THE POSITION OF THE POLICE FORCES

Although policemen have the duty to enforce the criminal law, and have wide powers to arrest, they are not servants of the Crown.[2] The Police Act, 1964, however, provides that a Chief Constable shall be vicariously liable for torts committed by constables under his direction and control. All police officers belong to one of the separate and independent police forces of the country. These are the county and area police forces, the City of London Police Force, and the Metropolitan Police Force. Only the last is truly controlled by the Crown as to matters of policy etc., for it is under the direct control of the Home Secretary, and the Crown appoints its Commissioner on the advice of the Home Secretary. Elsewhere the Home Secretary has the power to regulate concerning national conditions of service, which include wage rates, uniforms to be worn, pensions etc. The Police Act, 1964 also gives him power to call for a report upon any specific matter from a Chief Constable, to call upon a local police authority to require a Chief Constable, or his assistant or deputy, to retire in the interests of efficiency, and to cause a local inquiry to be held into the policing of any area. There has been a marked tendency in recent years towards amalgamation of more and more separate forces, which may well lead to increased efficiency and cooperation, and the Home Secretary's powers to instigate amalgamation were increased by the 1964 Act. Each police force

---

[1] See *e.g. Grant* v. *Secretary of State for India* (1877), 2 C.P.D.445. The position has not been affected by the Crown Proceedings Act, 1947, which will be discussed in Chapter 11, *post.*

[2] *A-G. for New South Wales* v. *Perpetual Trustee Co.*, [1955] 1 All E.R.846; [1955] A.C.457.

is under the control of a police authority, consisting as to two-thirds of members of constituent local councils and as to one-third of magistrates for the constituent areas. The Chief Constable in each case is appointed by the relevant police authority. The head of the City of London Police Force is a Commissioner appointed by the Court of Common Council of the City of London Corporation[1]. Nevertheless the Home Secretary maintains certain other indirect control of all the forces, because his approval is necessary for the appointment of any Chief Constable (or Commissioner of the City of London Police) to become effective. The granting of such approval is more than a mere formality, and in recent years approval has several times been refused in order to prevent a local man becoming Chief Constable: in the interest of preventing corruption etc. it is thought better that a stranger should be appointed. In addition, any constable or officer who feels himself aggrieved by certain decisions of his local police authority may appeal to the Home Secretary, who has the power to alter such decisions if he sees fit.

Grants are made from the Exchequer under statutory powers to local authorities for various services, including help for financing the local police forces, and it would be possible, though very rare, for any Home Secretary to exert pressure upon a local police authority by moving to suspend or reduce such payments for particular reasons.[2] Thus the Government may maintain some control over the police of the whole country, although full control is limited to the metropolis. The Report of the Royal Commission on the Police, issued in 1962, recommended that more responsibility should be given to the Central Government to promote co-ordination between police forces in the work of fighting crime and dealing with traffic, and the 1964 Act has carried out these recommendations. But Dr. A. L. Goodhart, in a powerful dissenting memorandum, considered that real efficiency in combating crime could only be achieved by the outright creation of a national force, regionally administered, with the Home Secretary responsible to Parliament for its proper maintenance and administration. It remains to be seen whether Dr. Goodhart's

---

[1] See Chapter 12, *post*.
[2] Such grants have been withheld four times since 1945: see B. Whitaker, *The Police* (1964), p. 91.

more radical views will ever triumph over the trend of cautious evolution which his colleages on the Royal Commission favoured.

VII. THE POSITION OF PUBLIC CORPORATIONS

It is not uncommon for a layman to believe that nationalised industries and monopolies are creatures of the Government. This is not necessarily so. Wherever an industry or undertaking has been put upon a national footing, with either a complete or a partial monopoly for one body to exercise, the practice has usually been to create a public corporation by Act of Parliament. Instances are the British Broadcasting Corporation, the National Coal Board, the British Airways Corporation and the British Railways Board. These bodies are incorporated by statute and become legal entities with much the same result as in the case of other companies or corporations. The Government very frequently retains the power to nominate or appoint some proportion of the directors or managers of these organisations, and there is no offer of investment facilities for the general public, but they are fully liable (unless the creating statute provides otherwise, which is rare) both criminally and civilly, and they do not normally become servants or agents of the Crown. Their statutes usually provide that reports and accounts are to be submitted to Parliament every year, and in this way Parliament retains some direct control over their affairs, and may decide upon the appropriate sums of money to be voted to them for future operations. But no Minister is responsible for the day-to-day running of public corporations, and this means that Ministers may not be asked questions about such matters in Parliament.

VIII. THE ROYAL PREROGATIVE

One last topic remains to be considered in this chapter. The Prerogatives of the Monarch have always been recognised by the courts in much the same way as they have recognised Parliamentary privilege.[1] Blackstone referred to the Royal Prerogative as "that special pre-eminence which the King hath, over and above all other persons, and out of the ordinary course of the Common

---

[1] See Chapter 2, *ante.*

law, in right of his regal dignity."[1] But since the Bill of Rights, 1689, there is little doubt that such Prerogatives as remain to the Crown exist by tacit permission of Parliament. So long as Parliament continues to allow the Monarch or the Crown (for most of the Prerogatives are now exercised only on the advice of the Monarch's Ministers) to retain any Prerogatives, then those Prerogatives will be pre-eminent, but they could always be swept away by Act of Parliament. But since the convention of advice upon which the Monarch acts leads to the placing of considerable extra power in the hands of the Government of the day, it would appear very unlikely that any Government party (or indeed any Opposition party, which in turn hopes to become the Government party) should wish to sweep them away. Parliament does, however, occasionally abridge, modify or replace such powers by statutory powers, as, for example, for defence purposes; and one notable instance of a partial abolition of a previously existing Prerogative was the passage of the Crown Proceedings Act, 1947, which will be discussed in Chapter 11. In a case of 1920,[2] Dicey's definition of the Royal Prerogative was approved: "the residue of discretionary or arbitrary authority, which at any given time is legally left in the hands of the Crown."

It is difficult to find a satisfactory division of the existing Prerogatives of the Crown, and it is in any case not intended to give an exhaustive list here, but perhaps the following classification will serve its purpose:

(a) Prerogatives which affect the person of the Monarch or the status of the Crown

These provide for the Monarch's personal immunity from legal action, that he is not affected by the general law concerning the disability of infancy, that the Crown is only to be affected by the passage of a statute if that statute concerns it expressly or must do so by necessary implication, and that on the death of one Monarch his successor immediately takes office.

(b) Prerogatives which are of wider implication

These may be of an executive, legislative or judicial nature, and it is convenient to divide them up accordingly.

---

[1] 1 Bl. Comm. 239.
[2] *A-G.* v. *De Keyser's Royal Hotel, Ltd.*, [1920] A.C.508.

(*i*) *Legislative.*—The Monarch summons, prorogues and dissolves Parliament, and he also gives the Royal Assent to legislation. He may legislate by Order in Council or by Proclamation (as explained above) for newly conquered or ceded colonies, until he has sanctioned a Constitution with a representative legislature in the colony.

(*ii*) *Executive.*—Many of these Prerogatives are mere relics of past days, but the more important include the following. The Monarch is technically head of all the armed forces. The Monarch appoints and dismisses Ministers,[1] civil servants, and officers and men of the armed forces. The Monarch creates peers and confers honours. The Monarch may create corporations by Royal Charter. In cases of national emergency the Crown is responsible for defence of the realm, and is the only judge of the existence of danger from external enemies.[2] The Crown may also, in time of war, requisition ships[3] and enter on private land to repel invasion,[4] although where a statute is applicable it must act under that, rather than under the Prerogative power.[5] In the field of foreign affairs the Royal Prerogative is perhaps most important of all, for it is within the Prerogative to declare war, make peace or enter into treaties, all without recourse to Parliamentary approval, although such approval will be required later if the rights of citizens are affected or the expenditure of public money is required. Foreign states, Governments or Heads of State may be recognised by the Crown, and the sending and receiving of diplomatic representatives is again within the Prerogative. A certain defence, known as the defence of "act of state", may be raised under the Prerogative power. It applies in cases where the Crown has done some act in relation to a foreign state or an alien enemy anywhere, or with respect to friendly aliens (*i.e.* citizens of foreign countries with which the United Kingdom is not at war) who are outside the Monarch's dominions. If such foreign state, alien enemy or friendly alien not within temporary allegiance brings an action against the Crown, the defence of "act of state" is a complete

---

[1] The Monarch, as has been observed above, still appoints the Prime Minister personally, but not the other Ministers.

[2] *R. v. Hampden* (1637), 3 State. Tr. 825.

[3] *The Broadmayne*, [1916] P.64, 67.

[4] *Case of the King's Prerogative in Saltpetre* (1607), 12 Co.Rep.12; *Burmah Oil Co. v. Lord Advocate*, [1964] 2 All E.R.348; [1965] A.C.75.

[5] *A-G. v. De Keyser's Royal Hotel, Ltd.*, [1920] A.C.508.

one, and the action must fail. This is also so where the act was committed by a servant of the Crown under orders, and even where the servant was not under such orders, but the Crown has chosen to "adopt" his act retrospectively.[1] No "act of state" defence is available to the Crown, however, in respect of acts committed by the Crown against a British subject anywhere.[2]

(*iii*) *Judicial.*—The Monarch is still technically the "fountain of justice", and the fiction still exists that he is present in *his* own courts, though the judges resolved as long ago as 1607[3] that he may not give an opinion on any case. In theory he normally prosecutes, and all writs are in his name. But it should be remembered that the judges of superior courts no longer hold office at the Monarch's pleasure.[4] Again the Monarch possesses the Prerogative of mercy, in that convicted persons may be pardoned or reprieved by Royal command, exercised through the Home Secretary.

From this brief sketch it may be seen that in theory the Prerogatives are numerous and wide, but very few of them are still exercised by the Monarch in person and according to his own discretion, and all exist only by leave of Parliament. In their present form they are of considerable practical use to any Government, and in particular the Prerogatives concerning foreign affairs are well-nigh essential for the proper functioning of our relations with other states. It may be that the term "Royal Prerogative" is itself unfortunate in the modern law as it leads some students to believe that the Monarch has more real power than is in fact the case. Perhaps "residuary executive power", or some such expression, might more accurately convey the present position. But the current terminology is a natural result of a monarchical establishment. Provided that it is remembered that "the Crown" usually means the whole of the executive, confusion should be eliminated. It is worth noting that the most important part of the Monarch's own personal share of the Royal Prerogative is also its most nebulous area of power, namely the right to advise and warn his Ministers, and to be consulted by them.

---

[1] *Buron* v. *Denman* (1848), 2 Exch.167.
[2] *Nissan* v. *A-G.*, [1969] 1 All E.R.629; [1970] A.C.179.
[3] *Prohibitions del Roy*, 12 Co.Rep.63, 64.
[4] See p. 41, *ante*, for the contrary position of Circuit Judges, Recorders and magistrates.

FURTHER READING

Sir W. Ivor Jennings, *Cabinet Government* (3rd ed., 1959).
Lord MacDermott, *Protection from Power under English Law* (1957), Chapter 2.
J. M. Hart, *The British Police* (1951).
Final Report of the Royal Commission on the Police, 1962, Cmnd. 1728.
B. Whitaker, *The Police* (1964).
G. Marshall, *Police and Government* (1965).
D. C. M. Yardley, "The Primacy of the Executive in England", (1968) XXI *Parliamentary Affairs* 155.

CHAPTER 4

THE JUDICIARY

Nothing more than the barest sketch of the system of courts and judges can be attempted in these pages, for the actual identity of the various courts is of little importance in the field of constitutional law. The power of the courts as a whole is what really matters in this respect, and the lawyer is entitled to expect that this power in any given instance will only be wielded by the court having the proper jurisdiction. Should the applicant for any remedy seek it in the wrong court it is the duty of such court to dismiss his application for that reason, and even if the court of first instance should fail to take this step there is always the possibility of appeal to a higher court upon this issue, or else, in the case of what are known as inferior courts, certain extraordinary remedies may be obtained to nullify the first proceedings. It will be noted that we are only concerned specifically with English courts in this chapter. The courts of Scotland and Northern Ireland are quite separate, as will be explained in Chapter 7 below, yet their powers as far as constitutional law is concerned are similar. It is intended in the present chapter, therefore, to consider first the constitutional position of all courts throughout the United Kingdom, and then to outline the nature of the various courts of law in England alone, the doctrine of precedent and the concept of judicial tenure. The English courts will thus be used as exemplifying a *system* which is common in all parts of the United Kingdom.

I. THE CONSTITUTIONAL POSITION OF THE COURTS

The primary function of the court is to determine the legality of various kinds of behaviour. This is not to say that it is open to any court to investigate an issue upon its own initiative. In each case it is for an individual to raise the matter as the subject of litigation in which he is involved, whether the issue is one of civil or of criminal law. In the field of criminal law most prosecution in England (the position is rather different in Scotland) is undertaken by the police or by the Department of the Director of Public Prosecutions, who is appointed by the Home Secretary to initiate prosecutions for murder and certain other crimes, under the control of the Lord Chancellor and the Attorney-General. But in some criminal cases and in civil cases of all kinds the litigation may be started by any private individual or by a corporation, as well as by the Crown. Indeed in theory it may be that the police really only undertake prosecutions as private individuals.

Once an issue has been raised in the appropriate court, it is for that court to reach its decision according to the law of the land. Not infrequently the law is regarded as certain, and the main problem in hand will be to determine the facts in the case before the court and then to apply the law to these particular facts. But sometimes there is doubt about the exact law upon a point, and it is then that the court has a discretion to make its own decision upon the nature of the legal rule involved. As has been seen above in Chapter 2, Parliament in its legislative capacity may introduce, alter or repeal any law it thinks fit, and in each case the effect will have been to formulate a new law for the future. Such law is absolutely binding upon all courts,[1] and the only discretion permitted to the courts is that of deciding how the law is to be applied to particular facts. But not all law is statutory. A large part of the law is "common law", in the sense of having been made by the decisions of courts, according to case-precedent where statute law has not yet encroached upon the particular field of law concerned. Although it would be realistic to consider this function as being legislative, yet it is more customary to regard it as adjudicatory upon the various opinions put before the court of what the law on a particular topic may or must be. In either event such decisions may always be overriden by a later Act of Parliament. Perhaps the only way in which it is at all possible for a court effectively to express its opinion upon a statute is by interpretation of the Act when it is arguable that more than one meaning may

---

[1] *Cf.* however the possible exception in Scots law, described at p. 35, *ante.* Northern Ireland courts are absolutely bound by Acts of the Westminster Parliament, but may declare Acts of the old Northern Ireland Parliament or the new Assembly invalid if made outside the powers of that body or in contravention of United Kingdom legislation: see Chapter 7, *post.*

be accorded to the wording of the Act which is in point. In one or two instances it has been known for courts to interpret statutes in such a way as in effect to flout the intention of Parliament,[1] but such instances are rare, and in any case cannot be blatant, for the bounden duty of the court is to apply the letter of the statute strictly, and in interpreting the meaning of a particular Act its only permitted object is to be able to enforce it once the meaning is discovered.

It will be seen, therefore, that the function of the courts is to discover and apply the law, and so to decide between the merits of arguments raised before them by exercising this function. The behaviour of the executive may be scrutinised by the courts upon these principles, and if necessary declared to be illegal, though certain exceptions to this general rule will be discussed later in Chapter 11. But it is never possible for the courts to question the validity of existing Acts of Parliament.[2] In this way the British Constitution differs from that of the majority of other countries of the world. Oddly enough the Constitution of the United States of America also differs upon this point from most other written Constitutions, for, although Article III vests the federal judicial power in the United States Supreme Court, there is no provision for any power to review legislative Acts of Congress. Yet such a reviewing power has been read into the Constitution by construction, and is now treated as beyond any doubt.[3] Any such Acts which do not conform to the provisions of the Constitution will be held invalid. In the United Kingdom all Acts of Parliament are treated as absolutely binding by the courts, regardless of whether they have any constitutional significance or not,[4] until such time as any particular Act is repealed or altered by Parliament itself in another statute.[5] Thus the courts, like all other institutions of the United Kingdom, have powers subordinate to the one most basic concept of the British Constitution, the sovereignty of Parliament.

---

[1] See the *Anisminic* case, discussed *supra*, p. 31.

[2] See, however, footnote 1, p. 52. As has been noted already in Chapter 2, no court is bound by any resolution of one of the Houses of Parliament which does not amount to a statute.

[3] See particularly the judgment of Chief Justice Marshall in *Marbury* v. *Madison* (1803), 1 Cranch 137; and Learned Hand, *The Bill of Rights* (1958), Lecture 1.

[4] See Chapter 2, *ante*.

[5] Or else by delegated legislation: see Chapter 10, *post*.

II. THE ENGLISH COURTS OF LAW

In this brief account it is convenient to divide the English courts into two groups, namely those which have a civil jurisdiction and those with a criminal jurisdiction.

A. *Civil courts*

The lowest courts in the hierarchy are the *magistrates' courts*, which have a limited jurisdiction over certain types of small civil disputes. The importance of these courts in civil cases is now, however, very minor. Most magistrates are unpaid Justices of the Peace (J.P.s), appointed and removable for each area by the Lord Chancellor on the advice of the Lord Lieutenant of the County (or by the Chancellor of the Duchy of Lancaster for that county). They are normally laymen, but they are assisted on points of law by the clerk of the court wherever they request his help, provided that he may never advise them on what their actual decision should be. Since 1966 there has been a short course of compulsory training for all new J.P.s. Appeals from magistrates' courts may be taken to the *Crown Court* or to a *Divisional Court of the High Court*, both of which courts will be described presently. If an appeal is taken to the Crown Court, a further appeal may lie to the Divisional Court later. Alternatively, the record of a case may be removed for review by the Divisional Court under the procedure of certiorari, which will be explained in Chapter 11.

County Courts have existed since 1846, when they were originally created by the County Courts Act. Their jurisdiction has been increased in scope several times since then, and now covers all types of minor civil disputes, with only a few exceptions. The factor which determines whether a dispute is minor or major is normally the pecuniary value of the subject-matter in dispute. Ordinary cases of contract or tort up to the value of £750 in dispute are usually brought in the County Court, though in other cases concerning, for example, recovery of land or probate, the limit is higher or lower according to the statutory provisions in force.[1] The judges appointed for County Courts are known as Circuit Judges, and they are appointed and removable by the Monarch on the advice of the Lord Chancellor. A jury may sit if

---

[1] The most recent statutes are the County Courts Act, 1959, the County Courts (Jurisdiction) Act, 1963, and the Administration of Justice Act, 1969.

either party wishes it where the sum claimed exceeds £5, though such a jury is rarely called upon in practice. In London the County Court retains the name of *Mayor's and City of London Court*. Appeals from decisions of County Courts lie, except in certain rare types of case, to the *Court of Appeal*, which is described below.

All other civil cases are heard in the *High Court of Justice*, which, together with the *Crown Court*, is part of the *Supreme Court of Judicature*, originally created by the Judicature Act, 1873, and now governed by the Supreme Court of Judicature (Consolidation) Act, 1925, and the Courts Act 1971. The High Court is divided into the *Chancery Division*, the *Queen's Bench Division* and the *Family Division*, each dealing for the most part with subjects for which it is best suited, although there is no strict rule that a case of any particular kind may only be brought in the appropriate Division and in no other. Generally speaking, however, most equity disputes appear in the Chancery Division, the primary business of the Family Division is implicit in its name, and the remainder of civil litigation appears in the Queen's Bench Division. Jury trial is now unusual in civil cases in the High Court, although it is still possible in certain types of dispute. The judges of the High Court are puisne Judges, appointed by the Crown on the advice of the Lord Chancellor. In addition, the Lord Chancellor is in strict law the president of the whole High Court and, more particularly, of the Chancery Division, of which latter Division the Master of the Rolls, appointed by the Crown on the advice of the Prime Minister, is another member; but in practice neither will sit in the High Court. The Vice-Chancellor is the senior judge normally sitting in the Chancery Division, and there is a President of the Family Division, while the Lord Chief Justice of England presides over the Queen's Bench Division. These latter judges are appointed by the Crown on the advice of the Prime Minister. For the hearing of cases at first instance the judges sit singly, and it is therefore usual in the High Court (and in the sittings of two or three judges in the Court of Appeal, discussed below) to find several judges sitting in different "courts" at the same time, each exercising the full power of the court. But for certain special purposes, such as the hearing of appeals from magistrates' courts, the judges of the High Court may sit in benches of two or three as a *Divisional*

Court of one or other of the Divisions, normally of the Queen's Bench Division. The High Court usually sits in London, but it may also sit in other parts of the country.

Appeals from the High Court or the County Court lie to the *Civil Division of the Court of Appeal*, the judges of which are the Lords Justices of Appeal, appointed by the Crown on the advice of the Prime Minister. They normally sit as a bench of two or three. The Lord Chancellor, the Lord Chief Justice, the President of the Family Division and the Lords of Appeal in Ordinary, are also members of the court, but in practice the president is the Master of the Rolls and only the Lords Justices normally sit with him.

The ultimate court of appeal in civil cases from English, Scottish or Northern Ireland courts is the *House of Lords*, where the judges are the Lords of Appeal in Ordinary ("Law Lords"), appointed by the Crown on the advice of the Prime Minister, who must have a quorum of three, but frequently sit as a group of five, and occasionally even of seven. Lay peers may not, by convention, sit when the House is hearing appeals, but any peers who hold or have held high judicial office may sit. The president is the Lord Chancellor. The House normally hears appeals in a committee room, and not in the legislative chamber. In certain special cases appeals in civil proceedings may go direct from the High Court to the House of Lords.

One modification of this entirely municipal system of courts is provided by certain Articles of the Treaties establishing the European Communities, which, since the European Communities Act 1972, now bind the whole of the United Kingdom. Where any question regarding the interpretation or validity of the European Treaties, or of the acts of the institutions of the Communities is raised before a court or tribunal of any member state, that court or tribunal may request the *European Court of Justice* to give a ruling thereon before proceeding further with the case in hand. And such a reference to the European Court must be made if there is no further judicial remedy against the ultimate decision of the court or tribunal concerned. Accordingly there will be some circumstances in which the House of Lords will be bound first to refer questions to the European Court. The judges of the Court of Justice are drawn from the member states, there being one from each state, plus one other.

At this stage the *Judicial Committee of the Privy Council* should also be mentioned, as it is the ultimate court of appeal from the courts of the Isle of Man, the Channel Islands, the various colonies and dependencies of the United Kingdom, and from the courts of such of the independent members of the Commonwealth as have not abolished the right of appeal to it.[1] The Committee also hears certain appeals from special tribunals, such as the General Medical Council, and gives advice to Parliament upon legal matter which may occasionally be referred to it.[2] The composition of the Board, as it is called, is often the same as for the hearing of appeals in the House of Lords, although Privy Councillors who are not Lords of Appeal are sometimes admitted to membership in view of their judicial experience in other Commonwealth countries. In recent years the membership of the Judicial Committee has been widened, and more Commonwealth judges have been appointed as Privy Councillors so that they might sit for the hearing of appeals. As has been pointed out in Chapter 3, all Lords of Appeal are Privy Councillors. The decisions of the Board are strictly speaking in the form of advice to the Crown, and only one "judgment" used to be given by the whole Board, but since 1966 it has been permissible for members to deliver dissenting opinions.

B. *Criminal courts*[3]

As before, the *magistrates' courts* are lowest in the hierarchy of courts, but they are of far more importance for the trial of persons charged with criminal offences than in civil proceedings, since they are responsible for the trial summarily of more than 95% of all accused persons. Such trial is of the persons accused of what may be generally described as the less serious offences. Because of the preponderance of this type of crime, particularly in large urban areas, stipendiary magistrates are sometimes appointed to relieve or take the place of J.P.s, and metropolitan stipendiary magistrates sit in the London boroughs. Specially qualified magistrates sit in *Juvenile Courts* with special powers. Although normally J.P.s sit as a bench of at least two, a stipendiary or metropolitan stipendiary

---

[1] Many independent countries have now abolished this right of appeal.

[2] See *e.g. Re Parliamentary Privilege Act, 1770*, [1958] 2 All E.R.329; [1958] A.C.331.

[3] It is not proposed to discuss the *coroners' courts* here, as they do not actually have the function of trying a case to reach a decision upon any particular person's guilt.

magistrate may sit alone and have the same powers as any two
J.P.s. Appeals from magistrates' courts in criminal cases lie, as in
civil cases, to the *Crown Court* and the *Divisional Court of the
Queen's Bench Division*. Any magistrate sitting alone also has the
power to examine a person who is accused of a more serious crime,
for he must decide whether there is a prima facie case to be
answered at a trial with a jury before that person may be committed
for trial. Only a magistrate may thus commit a person for trial for
an "indictable" offence.

The trial of all criminal offences of the graver variety is always
before a jury, and held in the *Crown Courts*. These courts, created
by the Courts Act, 1971, are held in various centres throughout
the country, and they are presided over by High Court judges,
Circuit Judges or Recorders, the latter being barristers or solicitors
appointed to act in this judicial capacity on a part-time basis.
There is also provision for J.P.s to sit with a judge. The Crown
Court in London retains the name of its predecessor, the *Central
Criminal Court*. Appeal from any conviction before a Crown Court
lies, at the instance of the defendant only, to the *Criminal Division
of the Court of Appeal*, which in any sitting consists normally of
either the Lord Chief Justice, a Lord Justice of Appeal and a
puisne Judge of the Queen's Bench Division, or a Lord Justice of
Appeal and two puisne Judges. The *Courts-Martial Appeal Court*,
composed in the same way as the criminal division of the Court
of Appeal, and first set up by statute in 1951, hears appeals
from conviction by courts-martial, but it is not necessary here to
consider the disciplinary powers of courts within the armed forces.

Once more the final court of appeal is the *House of Lords*. An
appeal lies, at the instance of either the defendant or the prosecutor,
from a decision of the criminal division of the Court of Appeal,
the Courts-Martial Appeal Court or the Divisional Court wherever
the court below certifies that a point of law of general public
importance is involved, and it appears either to that court or to the
House of Lords that the point is one which ought to be considered
by the House.[1] But, in distinction from its civil jurisdiction, the
House has no power to hear a criminal appeal from Scotland. The
Judicial Committee of the Privy Council hears criminal appeals from
jurisdictions outside the United Kingdom, but only where it

---

[1] Administration of Justice Act, 1960, and Criminal Appeal Act, 1968.

appears that there may have been grave mismanagement or a serious miscarriage of justice.

III. THE DOCTRINE OF PRECEDENT

The doctrine of *stare decisis*, which has been built up in England, and which is mirrored in Scotland and Northern Ireland, provides that decisions of the *House of Lords* are binding upon all lower courts and also usually upon itself. But in 1966 the Lord Chancellor, with the agreement of all the Law Lords, stated that the House of Lords would in future consider itself able to depart from any previous decision of the House when it appears right to do so. Subject to the overriding jurisdiction of the Lords, decisions of the *Court of Appeal* and of the *Divisional Court* are normally binding upon themselves and upon lower courts, but the qualifications upon this statement are too technical to explain in this book.[1] Decisions of the *High Court* or *Crown Court* are probably binding on inferior courts, but they are only highly persuasive upon later sittings of their own courts. All the courts that have been mentioned are regarded as "superior courts", except for the magistrates' courts and County Courts, which are "inferior courts". Decision of inferior courts do not bind other inferior courts, and they cannot even be regarded as highly persuasive. Any persuasive value which they possess at all is likely to be short-lived, as cases before these courts are not reported in any recognised series of reports.

The precedent value of any court decision is, of course, always subject to alteration by Act of Parliament.

IV. JUDICIAL TENURE

It is of particular importance that whereas judges of inferior courts may be removed from office by the Lord Chancellor (though this is a rare occurrence), all judges of superior courts, (that is, High Court judges and above) have the safeguard to their tenure of office that, although they must retire at the age of 75, they may in practice only be removed before that age by the Crown after an address requesting such removal by both Houses of

---

[1] See *Young* v. *Bristol Aeroplane Co.*, [1944] 2 All E.R.293; [1944] K.B.718.

Parliament.[1] Although it is sometimes alleged that it is undesirable that the judiciary should depend for their continued tenure of office upon the goodwill of the legislature, it is significant that over a period of 280 years no English judges have ever been so removed.[2] In addition the salary of all judges is charged on the Consolidated Fund, and it is not reviewed each year by the House of Commons with the other estimates of national expenditure.

FURTHER READING

H. G. Hanbury, *English Courts of Law* (4th ed., by D. C. M. Yardley, 1967).

G. R. Y. Radcliffe and Lord Cross of Chelsea, *The English Legal System* (5th ed., by Lord Cross of Chelsea and G. J. Hand, 1971).

A. K. R. Kiralfy, *The English Legal System* (5th ed., 1973).

O. Hood Phillips, *A First Book of English Law* (8th ed., 1970).

R. M. Jackson, *The Machinery of Justice in England* (6th ed., 1972).

R. J. Walker and M. G. Walker, *The English Legal System* (3rd ed., 1972).

K. J. Eddey, *The English Legal System* (1971).

---

[1] This was originally provided in the Act of Settlement, 1701, and the relevant statutes in force today are the Supreme Court of Judicature (Consolidation) Act, 1925, s. 12, and the Appellate Jurisdiction Act, 1876, s. 6 (concerning Lords of Appeal in Ordinary). A possible reserve power to dismiss, vested in the Crown alone, is discussed in, *e.g.*, Hood Phillips, *Constitutional and Administrative Law* (5th ed., 1973), pp. 334–335.

[2] It is, however, fair to add that some danger may exist where the British model concerning judicial tenure is copied in Commonwealth countries, where sometimes the political system is not yet as stable as in the United Kingdom.

CHAPTER 5

THE RULE OF LAW

Few phrases in recent years have become so well known by all members of the community as "the rule of law", and yet it is doubtful whether many of the people who commonly use the expression have more than a very vague idea what they mean by it. It is used most frequently by politicians and statesmen who essay to decry the actions of other political parties or foreign Governments on the ground that they do not measure up to the standards of common decency and fair dealing which they themselves believe they stand for. This use of the term is not incorrect, for it is not a technical expression, but it is certainly not a use which stems from any exact knowledge of its meaning; and as lawyers it is important that we should be able to define as far as possible the type of fair dealing to be regarded as the standard behaviour within the meaning of the expression. The most logical attempt in the sphere of international affairs that has been made to discover and explain the meaning of the phrase has been by the International Commission of Jurists, an independent international organisation, not set up by the United Nations, but enjoying consultative status with the United Nations Economic and Social Council. The purpose of the International Commission is to draw the attention of all Governments and peoples to any actions by any country or Government anywhere in the world which have the effect of curtailing the basic liberties of any members of the community.[1]

The activities of statesmen, and even of lawyers, in the international sphere are not, however, of any immediate significance in municipal British constitutional law. Yet the rule of law is still of some importance within that municipal law, and it is therefore our duty to investigate its nature and function. In doing

---

[1] Such basic liberties in the United Kingdom are discussed in Chapter 8, *post*.

so we must to some extent anticipate the contents of Part II of this book, for many developments in English administrative law have provided useful illustrations of the working of the rule of law. But it is best to leave consideration of the scope and details of administrative law until the basic principles of constitutional law have been explained. Many jurists through the centuries have been interested in the concept of the rule of law, but any modern discussion of the subject must begin with the theory of Professor A. V. Dicey, first published in 1885 in his *Introduction to the Study of the Law of the Constitution,* because discussion of the concept in this country has for the past eighty years centred round his ideas about the expression. Dicey divided the rule of law into three parts, explained by the following extracts:

(1) ". . . no man is punishable or can be lawfully made to suffer in body or goods except for a distinct breach of law established in the ordinary legal manner before the ordinary Courts of the land. In this sense the rule of law is contrasted with every system of government based on the exercise by persons in authority of wide, arbitrary, or discretionary powers of constraint . . . It means, in the first place, the absolute supremacy or predominance of regular law as opposed to the influence of arbitrary power, and excludes the existence of arbitrariness, of prerogative or even of wide discretionary authority on the part of the government."[1]

(2) ". . . every man, whatever be his rank or condition, is subject to the ordinary law of the realm and amenable to the jurisdiction of the ordinary tribunals."[2]

(3) ". . . the general principles of the constitution (as for example the right to personal liberty or the right of public meeting) are with us the result of judicial decisions determining the rights of private persons in particular cases brought before the Courts; whereas under many foreign constitutions the security (such as it is) given to the rights of individuals results, or appears to result, from the general principles of the constitution . . . Our constitution, in short, is a judge-made constitution . . ."[3]

It can be seen that the first two parts of the rule are closely allied, and may be said to amount to the concept of equality before the law for all citizens. The maxim *nullum crimen sine lege* would

---

[1] *Op. cit.,* (10th ed., 1959), pp. 188, 202.
[2] *Op. cit.,* p. 193.
[3] *Op. cit.,* pp. 195, 196.

be apposite here. It may be noted that the arbitrary rule of the
Nazi Government in Germany and elsewhere in the 1930s and
1940s, with the accompanying activities of the Gestapo, was in
clear breach of the first part of Dicey's rule, as are also the totalitarian acts of the many Communist Governments today. Dicey
did in fact go on to contrast English law with that of France, in
which country there existed (as there still exists today) a separate
system of administrative courts, which had jurisdiction over all
disputes between the state and individuals, to the exclusion of the
ordinary courts of law. Many critics of Dicey have believed that
he was asserting that no such thing as administrative law existed
in this country, but such criticism has been unjust, for he intended
to say no more than that we had no separate *droit administratif*
with its own special courts. As was clear to him and to all English
lawyers, there must always be a branch of law amounting to
administrative law, because no country can survive without an
administration, and any such administration must possess certain
legal rights, powers and duties which impinge in some way upon
the lives and rights of the ordinary citizens of the land. Dicey did
in fact publish a paper in the *Law Quarterly Review* in 1915,
entitled "The Development of Administrative Law in England",[1]
and it is now clear that he only intended to declare that in this
country the ordinary courts had jurisdiction over questions of
administrative law, just as over all other branches of the law, whatever the rules of those branches may be. Where he was wrong was
in believing that the French system favoured the state to the
detriment of the rights of the ordinary citizens of France, and that
thus the existence of the administrative courts was in conflict with
the rule of law. If one accepts Dicey's distinction between the
two systems as correct, with the exception of his mistaken distrust
of the French administrative courts, and that the ordinary courts
deal with English administrative law problems, then there is one
way at least in which the laws of the United Kingdom may have
progressed away from the concept of the rule of law since the time
of his writing, for, as we shall see in Chapter 11, a large number of
administrative tribunals have been created since his time, and
these tribunals have jurisdiction over much litigation of all kinds in
the field of administrative law. Their existence may be strictly

---

[1] 31 L.Q.R.148.

contrary to Dicey's first branch of the rule, but at least none of them ought to favour the executive to the derogation of the rights of individuals, and all are subject to control by the ordinary courts of the land, as will be explained in Chapter 11.

It is not hard to find a number of other examples in our laws which must be exceptions to the first two branches of Dicey's concept. Foreign sovereigns and diplomats enjoy special immunity from criminal prosecution or civil action, and judges can never be held civilly liable for anything done or said in the course of their office. Members of both Houses of Parliament enjoy extensive privileges, which have already been discussed in Chapter 2, while peers are disqualified from voting in Parliamentary elections. Trades Unions occupy a specially privileged position in that they cannot be rendered liable in tort at all,[1] although this legal immunity was only conferred for the first time by the Trades Disputes Act, 1906, some twenty years after Dicey first published his theory. Police powers of arrest without warrant may be regarded as infringements upon individual liberty, even though they are unlikely to be used in an entirely arbitrary manner in this country.[2] Discretionary powers may always be conferred upon the excutive, or indeed upon anyone, by Act of Parliament, the most usual example being the power to make delegated legislation,[3] and powers of a somewhat similar nature may be conferred also by the Royal Prerogative.[4] But at the time of Dicey's writing probably the most glaring exception from his rule was the immunity from the ordinary process of law which had been accorded to the Crown as a result of the Royal Prerogative, an immunity in which Parliament had acquiesced, for it could be useful to the Government or to any future Government. As we shall see in Chapter 11, this exception has been largely eliminated by the passage of the Crown Proceedings Act, 1947, and it is now true to say that in one very important respect our law has approached more nearly to the concept of the rule of law which Dicey had propounded.

It would be impossible to iron out all the inequalities. Perhaps

---

[1] For a powerful condemnation of the present Trade Union immunity, see Lord MacDermott, *Protection from Power under English Law* (1957), Chapter 7; and see the Industrial Relations Act, 1971.
[2] See Chapter 8, *post*.
[3] See Chapter 10, *post*.
[4] See Chapter 10, *post*.

the most clear example of all inequalities which are essential in civilised communities is provided by the age of criminal responsibility. It is unthinkable that a new-born baby or a very young child should bear full criminal responsibility for his activities. So the rule of law, even for Dicey, cannot have meant equal *treatment* for all before the law. It is enough that the same law covers us all, even though it makes different provisions for different groups of people—and it is of course always possible for the ordinary citizen to join a Trade Union or to become an M.P. Yet the fact that the various exceptions within the law may be recognised by the law in a totalitarian state is not enough to satisfy the principle of the rule of law. As the International Commission of Jurists has repeatedly stressed, a legal system must also provide for a proper balance, with judicial safeguards, between the interests of the state and of individuals, an independent judiciary and Bar, and social institutions allowing for the dignity of man.

The third branch of Dicey's rule is largely true, provided it is accepted that the concept of the sovereignty of Parliament is based on the decisions of the courts to that effect. Certainly it is true that the Constitution is part of the ordinary law of the land, and is not contained in any special instrument or instruments. The sovereignty of Parliament has been discussed already in Chapter 2, and we need not elaborate upon it further here, but its very existence renders the first two branches of Dicey's rule subject to a possible enormous practical exception.

The great value of Dicey's work in this field has been to provide lawyers and jurists with an ideal. It is not possible to formulate a satisfactory definition of the rule of law, and indeed it cannot seriously be contended that any one "rule" as such has any place in the law of the United Kingdom, which depends primarily on the rules laid down by Parliament and secondarily upon the concrete decisions of the courts. If such a theoretical "rule" has no place among the detailed statutes and decisions from which our law is drawn, then it cannot be considered as a basic tenet of our constitutional law. But as a guide to law-makers and reformers it can be of inestimable value, and for this purpose it is of little importance whether one accepts the views of Dicey or of any other jurist,[1] or constructs an entirely new idea concerning its

---

[1] See, *e.g.*, E. C. S. Wade and G. Godfrey Phillips, *Constitutional Law* (8th ed.), Chapter 5.

identity. Providing the aim is the preservation of the liberty and
rights of all members of the community, and that only such exceptions from this aim are allowed as are essential to the administration
of the nation in an orderly fashion (such as judicial and Parliamentary privilege, with proper safeguards), the purpose of the rule of
law will have been fulfilled. In short, the rule of law is not a rule or
a law, but a persuasive guide for the legislature, the executive and
the judiciary, linked in practice, in the United Kingdom, with the
working of many of the conventions which mitigate the theoretical
deficiencies in the Constitution, and mould it into a living democratic entity.

FURTHER READING

A. V. Dicey, *Introduction to the Study of the Law of the Constitution*
(10th ed., by E. C. S. Wade, 1959).
Sir W. Ivor Jennings, *The Law and the Constitution* (5th ed., 1959).
The various publications of the International Commission of
Jurists.

CHAPTER 6

THE DOCTRINE OF THE SEPARATION
OF POWERS

It is submitted that the three basic and essential functions in the administration of any independent state are legislative, executive and judicial. From a realisation of this generally accepted opinion has sprung at various times and in different countries the idea that the agencies through which these functions are exercised should be kept separate from each other, the intention being to prevent the concentration of more than one of the powers in any single authority, which might lead to tyranny, and to make sure that the due exercise of each is in no way hindered by the agencies responsible for the other two. Theories concerning the best methods of carrying out this intention go back as far as Aristotle, and find expression in the Constitutions of many nations, although in no country is the doctrine practised in such a way as to render the three functions entirely exclusive.

The Constitution of the United States of America, which came into effect on March 4th, 1789, probably provides us with the most extreme example of a practical separation of the three fundamental powers.[1] It is based upon a mistaken interpretation by the French writer Montesquieu of the position in England in the eighteenth century,[2] though it should be added that the founding fathers were interested in Montesquieu's views as applied to America, and they were in no way concerned about whether or not he had interpreted the English Constitution of his time accurately. The first three Articles of the United States Constitution vest federal legislative powers in Congress, the executive power in the President, and the judicial power in the

---

[1] The Constitution of the State of Massachusetts may possibly be more extreme in some respects.

[2] *De l'Esprit des Lois*, Chapter VI, paras. 3–6. In fact, as Madison pointed out in *The Federalist*, Montesquieu was mainly concerned to warn against the dangers of monopoly of power, and he may therefore have been less mistaken than is sometimes asserted.

Supreme Court of the United States. These powers appear to have been intended for the most part to be mutually exclusive, so that no member of one branch of government may be a member of either of the others as well, but even so the separation was not complete, and various "checks and balances" between the three agencies were provided. Thus, the President is empowered to veto legislation of Congress, and such a veto may be overriden by a two-thirds majority in each House of Congress. Any treaties which the President enters into with other countries must be ratified by a two-thirds majority in the Senate before they may come into effect. Although the normal rule is that no member of the Government may also be a member of Congress, yet the Vice-President *ex officio* presides over the Senate. The President appoints judges to office in the Supreme Court, and finally, even though there is no provision for this in the Constitution itself, it has been found essential that the Supreme Court should have the power to declare Acts of Congress (or of any State legislature) or actions of the President illegal if they should in any way transgress the provisions of the federal Constitution.[1] The system in the United States has justly been described as a separation of powers modified by checks and balances.

Turning to the United Kingdom, it is clear that the three fundamental powers exist, just as they exist in other countries, and they have been described in Chapters 2, 3 and 4 of this book. The legislative power is vested in Parliament, the executive power in the Crown, and the judicial power in the courts of law. In the earlier chapters we have endeavoured to point out both the existence of these basic functions and also their essential differences in nature, but it has become apparent that there is much overlapping between them and between the authorities in which the powers are vested. This is therefore the place at which to summarise the principal factors which in the United Kingdom render it impossible to insist that any strict separation of powers exists. As in the last chapter, it will be necessary in part to refer forward to certain material included in the later chapters of the book, but it is thought best to provide a complete picture of the position at this earlier stage.

---

[1] For a short but stimulating discussion of this topic, see Learned Hand *The Bill of Rights* (1958). See also Chapter 4, *ante.*

(1) Members of the Government are usually members of one or other of the Houses of Parliament, because it is desirable that all Ministers of the Crown should be held responsible to Parliament for their actions.[1] This is not an absolute rule, as may be seen from the case of Sir Frank Soskice, who was defeated in his constituency at the 1950 general election, but nevertheless retained his Ministerial position as Attorney-General, being elected to the Commons in a bye-election when another member of the Labour Party stood down from his own seat; or of Mr. Gordon Walker, who became Foreign Secretary in the Labour Government which came to power in 1964, despite his own defeat at the general election of that year, and who only resigned that office after his defeat at a later bye-election. Probably a member of the Government may retain his office providing he does not cease to be a member of one of the Houses of Parliament for more than a few months. It is, however, more usual for any Minister who takes office without possessing a seat in either House to be created a peer so that he may sit in the Lords. It may be noted that one of the most useful methods of checking up on the activities of Ministers or of the Government as a whole is the Parliamentary question: there is no such parallel possibility in the United States, where members of the Government do not sit in Congress, and there is no "question time". The concept of Ministerial responsibility to Parliament has been copied in the Constitutions of most independent Commonwealth countries.[2]

(2) The Monarch, who heads the Government, also in effect forms the "third House of Parliament".[3] Both this point and the last one lead to the common usage of "Parliament" and "Government" as interchangeable terms, although such a practice is of course incorrect. It will be recalled that the Government, through its Parliamentary majority, holds the whip-hand in the House of Commons, and thus can always force legislation through that House, and ultimately through Parliament as a whole.[4]

(3) The Monarch is the "fountain of justice", being technically present in all his courts of law, responsible for many

---

[1] See Chapters 2 and 3, *ante.*
[2] See Chapter 13, *post.*
[3] See Chapter 2, *ante.*
[4] See Chapters 2 and 3, *ante.*

judicial appointments, and exercising the prerogative of mercy in respect of persons convicted in the courts.[1] Thus he plays a part in all three of the fundamental powers.

(4) Parliament is strictly called the "High Court of Parliament", and although the House of Commons carries out no judicial functions today, the House of Lords is still the ultimate court of appeal.[2] The Lords of Appeal in Ordinary sit in the House of Lords both as a legislative body and as a court, and they are also Privy Councillors, as is indeed the Speaker of the House of Commons.[3] The Lord Chancellor also plays a part in all three of the powers, being a member of the House of Lords as a legislative body and as a court, responsible for a number of judicial appointments, and also a member of the Government.

(5) Although the independence of the judiciary is in practice jealously preserved,[4] superior judges are appointed by the Crown or by the Lord Chancellor, and are removable by the Crown on an address by both Houses of Parliament to the Crown, while inferior judges are appointed and removable by the Lord Chancellor.[5]

(6) The power to make delegated legislation is usually vested by Act of Parliament in the Government.[6]

(7) Administrative tribunals, as well as many of the ordinary courts of law,[7] are created either directly by Act of Parliament or by delegated powers conferred upon Ministers by statute. Their powers and duties may be both judicial and administrative.[8]

(8) Justices of the Peace are primarily judges, but still retain certain administrative duties, such as licensing.[9]

(9) Local government powers are created by Parliament or by Royal Charter, and are both legislative and executive within the district of each local authority.[10]

---

[1] See Chapters 3 and 4, *ante.*
[2] See Chapters 2 and 4, *ante.*
[3] See Chapters 2, 3 and 4, *ante.*
[4] See Chapter 4, *ante.*
[5] See Chapters 3 and 4, *ante.*
[6] See Chapter 10, *post.*
[7] See Chapter 4, *ante.*
[8] See Chapter 11, *post.*
[9] See Chapter 4, *ante.*
[10] See Chapter 12, *post.*

Enough has been said to show the interrelation between the three fundamental powers. It is very probable that the overlapping of powers and authorities insures against arbitrariness. It may be added, finally, that the all-powerful position of Parliament makes it possible for the legislature to make any alteration in the present system which it may wish by simple Act of Parliament. This is not only the method of passing ordinary legislation in the United Kingdom, but it is the procedure for effecting any constitutional amendment whatever.[1]

FURTHER READING

C. S. Emden, *Principles of British Constitutional Law* (1925).
B. Schwartz, *American Constitutional Law* (1955).

---

[1] See Chapter 2, *ante.*

CHAPTER 7

SCOTLAND, NORTHERN IRELAND,
THE ISLE OF MAN AND THE CHANNEL ISLANDS

In the present chapter it is intended briefly to sketch the importance so far as British constitutional law is concerned of those other parts of the British Isles which are not automatically subject to the municipal law of England and Wales. The relationships between each of these countries have already been mentioned in Chapter 1.

I. SCOTLAND

The separate Kingdoms of England and Scotland became associated by the personal union of the Crowns of both countries when James VI of Scotland succeeded to the throne of England as King James I in 1603, but the complete unification of the two countries in a political sense did not occur until the Treaty of Union, which was ratified by Acts of the two Parliaments of England and Scotland in 1707. The effect of the Treaty and Acts was to abolish the two Parliaments and to form a new Parliament of Great Britain, and thus ultimately a Government of the whole country, in Westminster. This position has been altered by the later union with Ireland, discussed below, only to the extent of increasing the jurisdiction of Parliament to cover the whole of the newly formed United Kingdom, and the full legislative authority of Parliament over both countries remains.[1] It has, however, remained customary to appoint six or seven members of each Government to special responsibility over Scottish affairs, and in particular there is always a Secretary of State for Scotland.

The Scottish courts of law, legal professions and legal system

---

[1] With the possible exception exemplified in the case of *MacCormick v. Lord Advocate*, 1953 S.C. 396, discussed in Chapter 2, *ante*.

have not been affected by the union, except in so far as Parliamentary authority was transferred to Westminster, and that the House of Lords became the ultimate court of appeal, though only in civil cases, as has been seen above in Chapter 4. The legal systems of England and Scotland have had widely different histories and traditions, but it is not our present purpose to examine them. The superior Scottish civil courts are the Inner and Outer Houses of the Court of Session, of which the Inner House, which sits in two Divisions, presided over by the Lord President and the Lord Justice-Clerk respectively, exercises appellate jurisdiction, while ten Lords of Session sit singly in the Outer House, as Lords Ordinary, to hear cases at first instance. The superior criminal court is the High Court of Justiciary, consisting of the same judges as the Court of Session but under the titles of Lord Justice-General, Lord Justice-Clerk and Lords Commissioners of Justiciary, which exercises both trial jurisdiction (one Lord with a jury) in Edinburgh or on circuit, and appellate jurisdiction. The inferior courts in both civil and criminal matters are the Sheriff Courts, held by sheriffs-substitute, from which appeals lie in civil cases either to the Sheriff Principal and then on to the Inner House of the Court of Session, or directly to the Inner House of the Court of Session, and in criminal cases to the High Court of Justiciary. The Scottish equivalent of the English Attorney-General is the Lord Advocate.

II. NORTHERN IRELAND

Northern Ireland is a part of the United Kingdom of Great Britain and Northern Ireland, as has already be seen in Chapter 1. Its law, like that of England and Wales, is a common law system, in that it is derived partly from Parliamentary statutes and partly from case law decided in the courts of the land. Prior to the Act of Union with Ireland in 1800, the Parliament of Ireland had legislative authority over the whole of Ireland, although some authority was at times claimed by the Parliament of England (up till 1707) and by the Parliament of Great Britain (between 1707 and 1800), for Ireland held the status of a lesser Kingdom under the English, and later the British, Crown. Between 1800 and 1922 only the Parliament of the United Kingdom of Great Britain and Ireland had this authority; and after the Irish Free State (Agreement) Act, 1922, which followed the partition of

Northern and Southern Ireland (the latter having since become the Republic of Ireland, and separate from the British Crown), the legislative power over Northern Ireland was held partly by the United Kingdom Parliament in Westminster and partly by the Northern Ireland Parliament at Stormont.

The Constitution of Northern Ireland, as laid down in the Government of Ireland Act 1920, involving the partition of Ireland and the creation of the Stormont Parliament, was always a matter of contention and gave rise from time to time to extremist action of a violent nature. As a result of a particularly serious wave of disorder and terrorism starting in 1969, the British Parliament prorogued the Stormont Parliament by the Northern Ireland (Temporary Provisions) Act, 1972, and imposed direct rule over the province from Westminster, such rule being exercised by a new Secretary of State for Northern Ireland. The Government made it clear at the time that it was intended as soon as possible to make further provisions for devolution of power to the province, and these provisions are now contained in the Northern Ireland Assembly Act, 1973 and the Northern Ireland Constitution Act, 1973, which also includes a charter of human rights for the province.

Under the 1973 Acts, a new Assembly, consisting of seventy-eight members, replaces Stormont, and the first elections to this Assembly took place in June 1973. In view of the fact that the Unionist Party had been in the majority in Stormont continuously from 1922 to 1972, and that no other party had been able to take part in the formation of the Northern Ireland Executive, it is now provided that elections are by a type of proportional representation, so that the proportion of members of the various political parties in the Assembly will largely mirror the number of votes cast for the parties at the preceding election for the Assembly. The Executive also, when formed, must consist of members of both the majority and minority groups. The Act does not stipulate how the mixed Executive should be set up, but appointments are made by the Secretary of State for Northern Ireland, who must be satisfied that the Executive is likely to be widely accepted throughout the community before he makes such appointments. The Executive, headed by a Chief Executive Member, who is also leader of the Assembly, has a maximum of twelve members, two of whom need not be members of the Assembly. If there is

no hope after an election of forming the necessary mixed administration, the Secretary of State may ask the Monarch to dissolve
the Assembly and order fresh elections.

The powers of the Assembly are similar to those formerly
possessed by Stormont, save that matters concerning law and
order are for the time being reserved for the Westminster Parliament. The Assembly may legislate on such matters with the
approval of the United Kingdom Government, and there is
provision for powers in this field to be transferred to the Assembly
in appropriate circumstances. The Assembly has exclusive powers
over many matters of great importance, such as agriculture, education, health and social services; but a number of excepted matters
are outside the competence of the Assembly, and solely within
the jurisdiction of Westminster. These exceptions include foreign
affairs, defence, elections, the appointment of magistrates and
judges, and some taxation. The Secretary of State will also continue to hold a wide range of intervention powers, including the
right to recommend to the Monarch that it is in the interests of
the public to dissolve the Assembly, and the right to seek the
view of the Judicial Committee of the Privy Council on whether
a particular measure of the Assembly is discriminatory. It should
be noted that whereas statutes of the United Kingdom Parliament
have sovereign authority throughout the whole of the United
Kingdom, the Northern Ireland courts have always had the power
to adjudicate upon the constitutionality of enactments of the
Stormont Parliament or of the Assembly by comparing any
legislation in question with the powers vested in the local legislature
by the Constitution of the province, or with existing statutes of
the United Kingdom Parliament.

The 1973 Act leaves untouched the arrangements whereby
twelve M.P.s are elected in Northern Ireland constituences for
the House of Commons at Westminster, where they possess equal
powers and status with members elected from other parts of the
Kingdom.

The law of Northern Ireland, although strictly an entirely
separate system from that of England, is in practice very like it,
partly because of the long history of close association, and later
actual union, with the mother country, and partly because its
legal development today tends to mirror that of its British partner.
The courts of Northern Ireland are very like those of England.

Thus there is a Supreme Court of Judicature of Northern Ireland, consisting of a High Court and a Court of Appeal, which sits in Belfast. There is also a Court of Criminal Appeal. Further appeals from the Court of Appeal in civil cases and from the Court of Criminal Appeal (in the latter case only under similar conditions to those which exist in England) lie to the House of Lords at Westminster, which in such cases must act as the highest court of appeal for purposes of Northern Ireland law. The officers and judges of the Northern Ireland courts bear similar titles to those of their English counterparts.

III. THE ISLE OF MAN

The Isle of Man is a separate dependency of the British Crown, and is not part of the United Kingdom, although Acts of the United Kingdom Parliament will apply to the island provided they do so expressly or by necessary implication. The legislature, one of the oldest in the world, is called the Court of Tynwald, and it is composed of the Lieutenant-Governor, the Legislative Council and the House of Keys. The Lieutenant-Governor presides over the Legislative Council, the other members being the Bishop of Sodor and Man, the First Deemster, the Attorney-General, and seven members elected by the House of Keys. The House of Keys consists of twenty-four elected members, and there must be a fresh election at least every five years. The Tynwald is responsible for most internal legislation, which must receive the Royal Assent, but certain important subjects, such as air navigation and merchant shipping, are usually dealt with by the United Kingdom Parliament.

The executive authority is vested in the Lieutenant-Governor, who is responsible, among other things, for defence, but in recent years he has been assisted by an Executive Council. The Royal Assent to legislation of the Tynwald is normally signified through the Lieutenant-Governor.

The law of the island, known as "breast law", is quite distinct from English law, though it tends more and more to resemble the latter today. The courts of the island are also distinct, and the judges are called Deemsters. The most important courts are the Staff of Government, which deals with civil cases, and the Court of Criminal Appeal, from either of which a further appeal lies to the Judicial Committee of the Privy Council.

IV. THE CHANNEL ISLANDS

The Channel Islands may in a sense claim to have been older dependencies of the English Crown than any other parts of the present British Isles, for they belonged to the Dukes of Normandy before England was annexed to the Duchy. The two main islands are Jersey and Guernsey, Alderney and Sark being dependencies of the latter. Although the islanders in theory deny the right of the United Kingdom Parliament to legislate for them, in practice they do not dispute it, and United Kingdom legislation is frequently extended to the islands by order in Council. The laws of the islands are of Norman origin, and are distinct from those of England. A word or two should be said about each island:

(1) *Jersey*

The local legislature is the States of Jersey, consisting of the Bailiff, who is nominated by the Crown and who presides, the Attorney-General, Solicitor-General, the Dean of Jersey, twelve senators, who are elected for nine years, twelve constables or mayors of the parishes and twenty-eight deputies, who are elected for three years. The Royal Assent is necessary before any legislation may come into force. The Lieutenant-Governor and certain island officials hold executive authority, and the Royal Court, presided over by the Bailiff or Deputy Bailiff, hears both civil and criminal cases, there being an appeal to the Court of Appeal for the Channel Islands, and a further appeal to the Privy Council in civil cases and also, with special leave of the Privy Council, in criminal cases where there may have been a grave miscarriage of justice.

(2) *Guernsey*

The institutions of the Bailiwick of Guernsey are mainly similar to those of Jersey. The States, however, consists of the Bailiff, Attorney-General, Solicitor-General, twelve conseillers, thirty-three elected People's Deputies and twelve elected douzeniers.

Alderney, although a dependency, maintains its own legislature, consisting of a President and nine members, all elected. *Sark,* another dependency, remains a feudal seignory, under the titular control of the hereditary Seigneur or Dame of Sark. Its legislature is the Chief Pleas, consisting of the Seigneur, the Seneschal, who is appointed by the Seigneur with the approval of the Lieutenant-Governor of Guernsey, twelve elected deputies and the forty tenement holders.

FURTHER READING

G. W. Keeton and D. Lloyd, with specialist contributors, *The United Kingdom, The Development of its Laws and Constitutions: Part I. England and Wales, Northern Ireland and the Isle of Man* (1955).

T. B. Smith and L. A. Sheridan, *The United Kingdom, The Development of its Laws and Constitutions: Part II. Scotland and the Channel Island* (1955) (replaced, so far as Scotland only is concerned, by Professor Smith's later book: see below).

T. B. Smith, *Scotland: The Development of its Laws and Constitution* (1962) (also published in Scotland as *A Short Commentary on the Law of Scotland*).

H. Calvert, *Constitutional Law in Northern Ireland* (1968).

CHAPTER 8

RIGHTS AND DUTIES OF THE CITIZEN

In many written Constitutions the fundamental rights of the citizen are specifically set out in the constitutional document, as in the first eight and the fourteenth amendments to the Constitution of the United States of America, or, to take a modern example, in the earlier Articles of the Constitution of India, which came into force in January 1950. But of course this is not the case as regards the inhabitants of the United Kingdom, for we have no such constitutional document. It would, however, be unrealistic to consider that the citizens of a democratic state should possess no guarantees safeguarding their individual liberties, for such could only result from a recognition that the state was itself of a totalitarian rather than a democratic nature. Similarly it would be unrealistic to consider that the same citizens were under no corresponding duties to their fellow-citizens and to the nation as a whole. Nevertheless it is as well to remember that such individual rights and duties as do exist in the United Kingdom are always subject to the overall power of alteration or abolition by Act of Parliament, for, as we have already seen in Chapter 2, the most basic of all constitutional factors in the United Kingdom is the unrestricted legislative power of Parliament.

In recent years there has been some pressure of a political nature for the enactment of formal statutory civil rights for the United Kingdom. It is not without interest that in the Northern Ireland Constitution Act, 1973, there is for the first time a charter of human rights for the province, and that in particular it lays down that any legislation or executive action which is discriminatory on political or religious grounds is unlawful. Perhaps this could be a forerunner of similar legislation for the United Kingdom as a whole.

I. Rights of the Citizen in the United Kingdom

The declaration of rights of the citizen in the modern sense really dates from the latter part of the eighteenth century, when

the revolutions in America and France took place. The theorists
and politicians of both these countries borrowed their ideas from
the writings of Locke, who, after the Bloodless Revolution of
1688–1689, wrote about natural rights in his *Two Treatises of Civil
Government.* Blackstone in the mid-eighteenth century had also
lectured and written on the subject of the individual's fundamental rights,[1] and his influence was greatly felt upon the laws and
the Constitution of the United States.[2] The American Declaration
of Independence in 1776 and the so-called "Bill of Rights" (the
constitutional amendments mentioned above[3]) in 1791 provided
inter alia for the preservation of such fundamental rights as freedom of religion, speech, the press, peaceful assembly, and that
there should be no deprivation of life, liberty or property without
due process of law. The French Declaration of the Rights of Man
in 1789 covers very much similar ground, and a far more recent
example of such an instrument is provided by the Universal
Declaration of Human Rights, adopted by the United Nations
General Assembly in 1948, although it may well be felt that the
statesmen of some of the countries which supported the latter
Declaration did so with their tongues in their cheeks, and certain
International Covenants on Human Rights adopted by the
General Assembly in 1966. It should be noted that the Universal
Declaration of Human Rights has no legal force in any country
unless expressly adopted in its municipal law. The same may be
said of the European Convention for the Protection of Human
Rights and Fundamental Freedoms, drawn up in 1950, though
most Western European countries, including the United Kingdom
which subscribed to the Convention, undertook thereby certain basic
obligations and agreed to set up, where necessary, machinery for
the investigation of and adjudication concerning, the civil liberties
with which the Convention dealt. The acceptance by the United
Kingdom Government of the competence of the European
Commission of Human Rights has already been mentioned in
Chapter 2.[4] Its practical effect is that any United Kingdom
citizen who has exhausted his domestic legal remedies may apply

---

[1] *Commentaries on the Laws of England,* Vol. 1.
[2] See H. G. Hanbury, *The Vinerian Chair and Legal Education* (1958)
Chapter III.
[3] The first eight amendments apply to federal rights, and the fourteenth
amendment applies to the States.
[4] *Ante,* p. 34.

to the Commission for a remedy against the violation of any of the fundamental rights set out in the European Convention.

In England it is only possible to select certain statutes or charters as having the most significance constitutionally. These purport to perform somewhat similar functions, and include Magna Carta, 1215, the Petition of Right, 1627, and the Bill of Rights, 1689, all having appeared before the time of Locke's writings. None of these documents is really a statute in our modern sense, for they only amount to the acceptance by the Monarch of certain demands by Parliament or his people. But they have always been treated as of statutory force. The latter two documents were mainly concerned with the freedom of Parliament in the face of the power of the Monarch rather than with the individual liberties of each citizen, and Magna Carta primarily protected the privileges of the barons, but it is the spirit of English law to discover general principles from particular instances.[1] Although there is no need in the present work to examine the documents closely, many basic freedoms have been deduced from them and also from the representative character of Parliament, which, it is argued, would not be permitted by the electorate to exercise such extreme legislative authority unless it did so primarily as a means of protecting and safeguarding the lawful interests and freedoms of the populace. It is therefore assumed that basically all citizens are free to do and act as they please, and that this liberty will only be curtailed in so far as such limitation may be essential for the due and just administration of the whole country, and then only by law and not by arbitrary power. The stability of British institutions, strengthened by the good fortune of centuries of steady growth, unhampered by foreign invasion, is enough to render otiose any more codified list of civil liberties. Even though some Prerogative powers cut across individual liberty, they only exist so long as Parliament permits them to remain in the interests of the community, as has already been pointed out in Chapter 3. Thus, as far as British constitutional law is concerned, our main task is to determine in what ways individual liberty is *restricted* by law, and not how it is preserved. We shall also, however, consider the remedies provided by law for the infringement of such

---

[1] See Roscoe Pound, *The Development of Constitutional Guarantees of Liberty* (1957), Chapters 1 and 2.

fundamental rights as citizens do possess. Our approach must be primarily negative, but for convenience we may assume that certain basic rights exist except where they have been curtailed by the law, whether statute or common law, and these rights may be said to be:

(1) freedom of the person to behave as he pleases,
(2) equality before the law,
(3) freedom of property,
(4) the right to free elections,
(5) freedom of speech and to write,
(6) freedom of public worship,
(7) freedom of assembly and association, and
(8) family rights.

It is possible that to this list may be added the right to work and the right to withhold one's labour.

Some limitations upon the foregoing list are obvious and need not be further explained. Thus freedom of speech and writing must of necessity be restricted by the law of defamation, which in itself is protecting other individuals from encroachment upon their own liberties by single individuals, and by the laws of sedition, censorship, contempt of court, obscenity, and the prevention of disclosure of official secrets. Freedom of property is subject to the levying of taxes, without which the administration of the country would collapse, and to statutory powers of compulsory acquisition. Again, equality before the law, a concept which has already been discussed in Chapter 5, is a rule with several important exceptions. As has been seen, judges and M.P.s must receive special protection from ordinary legal process so that they may carry out their duties efficiently, and the same largely applies to diplomats; whereas infants under the age of majority cannot be held fully responsible in law for all their actions.

But other exceptions to the basic freedoms require some explanation. The detailed limitations discussed in this chapter are rules of English law only, unless otherwise indicated, but the laws of Northern Ireland and Scotland are not very dissimilar.

A. *Incursions upon freedom of the person and property*

Every man is free to do as he wishes unless the law otherwise provides, as, for example, by the law of assault, or by the law making it an offence to drive a motor vehicle having consumed alcohol in such a quantity that the proportion in the blood, as ascertained by a compulsory laboratory test, exceeds the prescribed limit.[1] A different statutory limitation may be found in section 3 of the Trade Disputes Act, 1906, where it is provided that an act done by a person in contemplation or furtherance of a trade dispute shall not be actionable on the sole ground that it may interfere with the right of some other person to dispose of his capital or his labour as he wills. Thus, by implication, an individual may find his power to dispose of capital or labour hampered without being able to take action to re-establish his right so to dispose of it, unless the person interfering with his right has also offended against the law in some other respect, such as by being guilty of a conspiracy in furtherance of private vengeance.[2] He would of course, as was pointed out in Chapter 5, be powerless to redress the wrong if the additional offence amounts to a tort and it is committed by a Trade Union or Unions, or by Union members in contemplation or furtherance of a trade dispute, as is also provided by the Act of 1906.

Any arrest of a person must normally be with the authority of a warrant signed by a magistrate and executed by a police officer; and such a warrant will only be issued where the magistrate is satisfied that the grounds for the warrant are lawful. Warrants must name the individual to be arrested specifically, for it was held in 1765[3] that "general warrants" were illegal. In that case a warrant for the arrest of the authors, printers and publishers of "The North Briton" was held to be too general. One of the most celebrated of all English constitutional law cases is *Entick* v. *Carrington*, decided in the same year,[4] in which the plaintiff, who was suspected of being the author of "The Monitor; or British Freeholder," obtained £300 damages for trespass committed by Carrington and certain other King's messengers, who had broken and entered his house and seized his papers and books under a general search warrant issued by a Secretary of State. In petty cases accused persons are "summoned", and a warrant will only issue if the summons is disobeyed. Arrest without warrant by a

---

[1] Road Safety Act, 1967, Part I.
[2] See *e.g. Huntley* v. *Thornton*, [1957] 1 All E.R.234; [1957] 1 W.L.R. 321.
[3] *Leach* v. *Money* (1765), 3 Burr. 1749.
[4] (1765), 19 State. Tr. 1029.

police officer is permitted, *inter alia*, where he has a reasonable
suspicion that a person has committed a serious crime, and any other
citizen may arrest a person without a warrant where such crime has
actually been committed, or if he is called upon to assist a constable
or magistrate. There are also certain other special statutory
provisions for arrest without warrant which need not concern us
here other than to note that they exist.[1] Any person arrested
without a warrant must be told, either in technical or non-
technical language, the true ground of arrest. It is not sufficient
merely to state the general ground, such as "murder", unless the
circumstances are obvious, as when the accused has been caught
in the act of committing an offence. In a House of Lords case in
1947[2] two police officers were held liable for false imprisonment
after wrongfully arresting the plaintiff without a warrant and mis-
informing him as to the actual charge to be brought against him.

Police powers of search and entry

Although the normal rule is that no person may enter private
premises without permission from the owner or occupant, police
may always enter premises to execute a warrant for arrest or to
search a person lawfully arrested. It was also held in the famous
case of *Elias* v. *Pasmore* in 1934[3] that where police lawfully enter
private premises to arrest a man, but do not possess a search
warrant, they will still be excused if they take documents or search
the premises, provided that they discover something which is
useful as evidence in the prosecution of the arrested person, or
even of some other person altogether. This decision really provides
that documents, even though illegally seized, may be put in
evidence against an accused person.[4] But it may amount to a dan-
gerous accretion of power in the hands of the police, even though i

---

[1] One of the most recent examples is provided in the case of soliciting b
the Street Offences Act, 1959.

[2] *Christie* v. *Leachinsky*, [1947] All E.R.567; [1947] A.C.573.

[3] [1934] 2 K.B.164; [1934] All E.R. Rep. 380.

[4] An earlier case was *Jones* v. *Owen* (1870), 34 J.P.759. Later cases are *Kin*
v. *R.*, [1968] 2 All E.R.610; [1969] 1 A.C.304; and *Ghani* v. *Jones*, [1969]
All E.R. 1700; [1970] 1 Q.B.693. See also *R.* v. *Leathem* (1861), 8 Cox C.C.498
at p. 503, where Crompton, J. said: "It matters not how you get it; if you steal
even, it would be admissible in evidence." This statement was cited with approv;
by the Privy Council in *Kuruma* v. *R.*, *post*. For possible exceptions to this rul
see A.R.N. Cross, *Evidence* (3rd ed., 1967), pp. 266–268.

was made clear in the case itself that the accused would still have
a right of civil action against the police for trespass etc. in respect
of any documents searched or taken away which proved to be of
no use for a prosecution. This decision has to some extent been
superseded by the provisions in the subsequent Incitement to
Disaffection Act, 1934, and the Public Order Act, 1936, which
specify types of case in which it shall be lawful for the police to
make searches without warrant. It should be remembered that
many of the cases on this subject, and on that of police powers
in respect of unlawful assemblies etc., considered below, took
place in the economically and politically troubled times of the
1930s, when considerable difficulty was experienced in controlling
the public meetings and activities of Communists and Fascists.
Extensive powers were sometimes sorely needed.

But *Kuruma* v. *R.* in 1955[1] makes it clear that the statutes leave
untouched the basic common law provisions concerning ad-
missibility of illegally obtained evidence. In that case a Kenyan
had been found guilty under Emergency Regulations in force at
the time, of unlawfully possessing ammunition, and had been
sentenced to death. Although he had been lawfully arrested under
the Regulations, the policemen who arrested him had no power
to search him, since they were below the rank of officer (assistant
inspector) that had such a power to search without warrant in
Kenya. Yet the policemen who arrested him did search him at the
time of his arrest and they found two cartridges on him which
were used as vital evidence at his trial. On appeal to the Privy
Council, it was held that the use of such evidence was lawful; and
of course any question of a right of civil action for any part of the
search which proved useless for the purposes of a prosecution
would have been small comfort to Kuruma. The Board, however,
did direct that the sentence should not be carried out until the
Secretary of State had had an opportunity of considering the case.
A decision which possibly goes even further is *Chic Fashions
(West Wales), Ltd.* v. *Jones,*[2] in which the Court of Appeal held
that a constable who enters premises by virtue of a search warrant
for stolen goods may seize not only the goods covered by the
warrant, but also any other goods which he believes on reasonable

---

[1] [1955] 1 All E.R.236; [1955] A.C.197.
[2] [1968] 1 All E.R.229; [1968] 2 Q.B.299.

grounds to have been stolen and to be material evidence on a charge of stealing or receiving against the person in possession of them or anyone associated with him. It was further held that subsequent events cannot affect the lawfulness of the original act, so that the fact that the goods were not stolen, and not used as evidence on the prosecution of any criminal charge, did not render the Chief Constable liable in damages for trespass. It seems that a balance should be struck between protection of the individual from excessive police powers and the desirability of the police being able to use relevant evidence for a prosecution, however it is obtained. To take an extreme example, if a policeman chases a man he sees committing a theft, and in catching him happens to put his hand in the man's pocket, and then withdraws his hand which is (unlawfully) grasping a piece of paper, and this paper turns out upon inspection to be a written confession to a murder which the criminal had been carrying round with him for his own private delectation, it would be ridiculous to say that the policeman's only duty as far as the paper was concerned would be to return it and forget he had ever seen it. But on the other hand the police should not be encouraged to go to all sorts of unlawful lengths on the off-chance that some relevant evidence might turn up.

A further possibility of invasion of private premises by the police without warrant is instanced by the case of *Thomas* v. *Sawkins*,[1] which provides a limitation at common law upon the general right to hold a public meeting on private property. There it was held that the police may enter private premises without a warrant if they have reasonable grounds to believe that, if they are not present, seditious speeches will be made or breaches of the peace will take place. It appears, therefore, that a general licence to the public to enter private premises may be revoked as concerns anyone except a policeman, who may in his discretion override such a revocation. Such a police power is, however, limited, for it has also been held[2] that a power of entry without warrant does not exist where the commission or future commission of merely a summary offence has been suspected.

The cases considered above in this section are all cases at

---

[1] [1935] 2 K.B.249; [1935] All E.R. Rep. 655.
[2] *Davies* v. *Lisle*, [1936] 2 All E.R. 213; [1936] 2 K.B.434.

common law, but certain statutory powers of entry and search
have also been conferred upon civil servants, public corporation
officers, inspectors of gas and electricity meters, health visitors etc.

Emergency powers and martial law

Statutory emergency powers provide a further great infringement of personal and property freedoms. There is no need to
consider them in detail here, for each such power is conferred for
a particular purpose at a particular time, especially in war-time.
The powers are thus of many different kinds and depend entirely
upon the need which Parliament and the Government feel has
asserted itself at the time. They supplement, and in many ways
supplant, such Prerogative powers as exist to restrict individual
liberty in times of stress.[1]

Martial law means the suspension of ordinary law, and the
substitution therefor of discretionary government by the executive, exercised by the military. It is thought to be among the
Royal Prerogatives to be able to proclaim martial law, though only
in times of war. Such a power has not been exercised in England
since the time of Charles I, and it is arguable that the Prerogative
has been superseded by Parliamentary supremacy. Certainly it is
most unlikely that the Crown should attempt to declare martial
law, as Emergency Powers Acts are probably more efficacious.
The Crown has, however, sometimes set up military tribunals
under its Prerogative power when a state of war existed, as for
instance in Ireland in the early 1920s.[2] It is also conceivable that
the Parliamentary procedure might become impossible to work
in the event of, say, a nuclear attack upon London without warning,
but it might be more realistic to consider such a situation not as
one where the Prerogative power came into its own, but as one
where whoever was left alive would take upon himself the task of
trying to restore some order out of the wreckage.

Remedies for wrongful deprivation of liberty or property

Where there has been wrongful invasion of a person's liberty
or property he may have any of the following remedies:

[1] See Chapter 3, *ante; e.g. Case of the King's Prerogative in Saltpetre* (1607),
12 Co. Rep. 12.
[2] See *e.g. Re Clifford and O'Sullivan*, [1921] 2 A.C.570.

(1) a civil action for damages, such as for assault, false imprisonment, malicious prosecution, trespass to the person, land or goods etc.;

(2) a similar action for recovery of property;

(3) a criminal prosecution for assault, battery or theft etc.;

(4) a writ of habeas corpus to obtain his release from custody;

(5) perhaps a prerogative order to quash a proceeding wrongly taken against him;

(6) an appeal to a higher court, if the encroachment upon his liberty or property has been by court process; or occasionally

(7) the right to take out a summons before a magistrate to recover costs of defending irregular and unjustifiable proceedings.

Of these remedies, the prerogative orders will be discussed in Chapter 11, and only habeas corpus requires any further explanation here.

Habeas corpus

The prerogative writ of *habeas corpus ad subjiciendum* has for many centuries been one of the most important safeguards of individual liberty, and is still regarded as the ultimate weapon of defence for the oppressed.[1] The exact machinery and effect of the writ has been reformed by statute from time to time in order to ensure its full efficiency, the most notable of such statutes being the Habeas Corpus Acts of 1679 and 1816. An applicant for the writ must allege that he or the complainant is being unlawfully detained, whether it be for a criminal or civil offence, or for no offence at all (as, for example, where it is alleged that A is being prevented from leaving his own house by B). Frequently the application is made through an interested friend or relative of the imprisoned person. Possibly the use of the telephone also plays some part today. A prima facie case must be made out before the writ will issue, but if a superior court or judge grants the issue of the writ the effect is to cause the alleged captor to "bring the body" of the prisoner before the judge, who will then decide on

---

[1] It may perhaps be noted here that the right to habeas corpus has been suspended in Northern Ireland, where the executive has had certain powers of discretionary imprisonment, since 1939.

the merits of the case whether there is any legal ground for continuing to detain him. If no such legal ground is found to exist the applicant is set free by the court. Until recently, for example, it was not uncommon for persons detained in mental institutions to apply for the writ, and such applications were not infrequently successful because magistrates had exceeded their powers.[1]

If an application for the writ has been turned down, no second application will be entertained by any court in any circumstances on the same grounds unless fresh evidence is adduced. This rule was introduced by the Administration of Justice Act, 1960, to resolve certain doubts which had persisted up to that time. In the same Act the opportunity was taken to widen the rules concerning appeals, which had previously only been possible in civil cases. Although no appeal is permitted from the order of a single judge granting an application for habeas corpus in a criminal case, appeals *are* now permitted from any decisions of the Divisional Court, whether to grant or to disallow applications for the writ, and they lie, as in other criminal cases, direct to the House of Lords. But such appeals are not hampered by the necessity for the Divisional Court to certify that a case involves a point of law of general public importance which applies in other criminal appeals,[2] and so it is probably easier to appeal in a habeas corpus case than in any other criminal case. It is also provided that, although a single judge may grant an application for the writ, only the Divisional Court may refuse it, so that any single judge to whom an application has been made, and who is disposed to disallow it, must refer the application to the full Divisional Court.

B. *Incursions upon freedom of assembly and association*

Although the practice of meeting or demonstrating peacefully in public is common and not in itself unlawful, there are a number of criminal offences which reduce the general freedom of assembly

---

[1] Under the provisions of the Mental Health Act, 1959, these powers of magistrates have now in effect been surrendered to the medical profession. Two doctors, one of whom must have special psychiatric qualifications, are empowered to order a patient's compulsory detention in hospital for a period of either twenty-eight days or up to a year in the first instance. The patient has a right of appeal from such an order to a Mental Health Review Tribunal.

[2] See Chapter 4, *ante*.

and association. The offences to be considered in this section are
as follows:

(1) *Conspiracy*

A combination or agreement of two or more persons to do an
unlawful act, or to do a lawful act by unlawful means, is an
indictable offence at common law. Thus any assembly or association
which amounts to a conspiracy will be criminal. Such assemblies
must, however, be distinguished from the activities of Trades
Unions, which are legal associations with the principal object of
collective bargaining about wages and conditions of work.[1]

(2) *Affray*

Where two or more persons engage in a fight, whether in a
public place or on private premises, and thereby put other non-
participants in fear, they are guilty of the common law offence of
affray.

(3) *Unlawful assembly*

Where three or more persons either assemble to commit, or
when assembled do commit, a breach of the peace, or assemble
with intent to commit a crime by open force, or assemble for any
common purpose, lawful or unlawful, in a manner which gives
firm and courageous persons in the neighbourhood reasonable
cause to believe that a breach of the peace will occur they are
guilty of a common law offence.[2] The distinction between this
crime and that of conspiracy, apart from the requirement of
at least three persons to form an unlawful assembly, is primarily
that conspirators need not have caused any alarm to other people.

---

[1] Trade Union Act, 1871; Industrial Relations Act, 1971.
[2] See *e.g.* the judgments in *Humphries* v. *Connor* (1864), 17 Ir.C.L.R.1;
O'Kelly v. *Harvey* (1883), 14 L.R.Ir.105; *Wise* v. *Dunning*, [1902] 1 K.B.167;
cf. Beatty v. *Gillbanks* (1882), 9 Q.B.D.308, where it was held not to be an
unlawful assembly when the Salvation Army insisted on holding its normal
peaceful procession in Wester-super-Mare, even though they had been ordered
by the magistrates and the police not to do so because it was likely that it would be
broken up by a rival "Skeleton Army". It may be noted that the crime of obstruction of the police, discussed below, was not thought at the time to cover the
circumstances of a case where an assembly which the police wished to disperse
may not in itself be unlawful: see T. C. Daintith, "Disobeying a Policeman—
A Fresh Look at *Duncan* v. *Jones*," [1966] *Public Law* 248.

(4) *Rout*

A common law rout is committed where persons unlawfully assembled are actually moving forward to the execution of their purpose.

(5) *Riot*

A common law riot is committed where three or more persons, having a common purpose of a private nature, embark upon the execution of that purpose, with the intention of helping one another, by force if necessary, against anyone who may oppose them, and display such force or violence as to alarm at least one person of reasonable firmness and courage. Thus a riot may amount to the execution of the purpose of an already unlawful assembly.

(6) *Miscellaneous statutory offences*

It may be noted that the above crimes are usually committed in public places, and on this score they may be compared with police powers in respect of private premises, such as are exemplified in *Elias* v. *Pasmore*[1] or *Thomas* v. *Sawkins*,[2] discussed above. Various Acts of Parliament establish other offences, such as unlawful drilling, seditious meetings and tumultuous petitioning. Only two such offences need be mentioned specially here, namely the offence laid down by section 5 of the Public Order Act, 1936,[3] and consisting of offensive conduct conducive to breaches of the peace, and that of obstruction of the police, now governed by the Police Act, 1964, s.51.

Any person in a public place or at a public meeting who uses threatening, abusive or insulting words, or indulges in suchlike behaviour, or distributes or displays any writing, sign or visible representation of like effect, with intent to provoke a breach of the peace, or whereby a breach of the peace is likely to be occasioned, is guilty of an offence under section 5 of the Act of 1936. This section has been used by the police to prosecute those who publicly preach social hatred,[4] and the Public Order Act, 1963,

---

[1] [1934[2 K.B.164; [1934] All E.R. Rep. 380;
[2] [1935] 2 K.B.249. [1935] All E.R. Rep. 655;
[3] As amended by the Race Relations Act, 1965, s.7.
[4] See *e.g. Jordan* v. *Burgoyne*, [1963] 2 All E.R.225; [1963] 2 Q.B.744, 1045.

greatly increases the penalties which may be exacted by the courts. Provisions designed further to eliminate other aspects of racial discrimination are to be found in the Race Relations Acts, 1965 and 1968. Any person who wilfully obstructs a police officer in the course of his duty may be arrested without warrant. It is clear that this is a case where a policeman who has a suspicion that an unlawful assembly might take place can avoid having to wait and see, and can simply order the persons concerned to disperse. Any disobedience would then amount to obstruction.[1] But a decision in 1966 emphasizes that obstruction of a police officer is not unlawful unless it is also wilful.[2] The appellant had been seen by a police officer acting suspiciously late at night in a district where a number of breaking offences had been committed on the same night. On being questioned, he refused to give his full name and address, to say where he was going or where he had come from, or to accompany the officer to a police box in order that his identity might be established. The Divisional Court held that he was entitled to refuse to do all these things until he had been arrested, that "wilful" imported something done without lawful excuse, and that no obstruction without lawful excuse had been established in this case. Accordingly they quashed his conviction.

Once more the powers of the police are prominent as being the agency whereby the legal limitations are enforced. It will be noticed that, as before, much is left to the discretion of the individual police officer, and it may be argued that such exercise of discretion could be subjective. Police officers might be able to order law-abiding people to move away from a department store or a busy street for no apparent reason. Police are also much concerned with preventing and remedying traffic obstruction, and in enforcing local bye-laws,[3] in both of which occupations they are empowered to exercise a wide discretion. Again, an officer might arrest without a warrant because he believed the individual arrested had committed an offence or was about to do so, or he might enter private property where he believed a breach of the peace was likely to take place, whereas no other reasonable policeman would have drawn the same conclusion, and it might be argued that such an arrest or entry would nevertheless be lawful. This solution

---

[1] As happened in *Duncan* v. *Jones*, [1936] 1 K.B.218; [1935] All E.R. Rep.710;
[2] *Rice* v. *Connolly*, [1966] 2 All E.R.649; [1966] 2 Q.B.414.
[3] These are explained in Chapters 10 and 12, *post*.

would be undesirable, and although the point has not been decided directly it is probably correct to consider that belief in the commission or likely commission of an offence must be reasonable in the objective sense. Thus the policeman must behave as a "reasonable policeman".[1] If this principle is accepted there is little danger that the extensive police powers in this field of the law will ever be seriously abused.

C. *Offences against the state*

Any commission of a criminal offence amounts to an abuse of the limits of personal freedom permitted by the law, as also, in a different way, does the commission of any tort. It is not intended in this section to consider all criminal offences, but only those crimes against the state which are of such fundamental importance as to occupy a place in our constitutional law. Only three groups of these offences, treason, sedition, and offences against the Official Secrets Acts, need be discussed specially.

(1) *Treason*

The most important statute concerning treason is the Statute of Treasons, 1351, which is generally regarded as having been declaratory of the common law at the time, and which is still in force, although amended and added to in comparatively minor ways by subsequent Acts, primarily by statutes passed in 1702, 1707, 1795 and 1817. Under the Statute of Treasons the following types of conduct amount to the offence:

(a) Compassing the death of the King, the Queen or their eldest son and heir. An overt act is, however, necessary to prove the commission of this offence.

(b) Violating the King's consort, or eldest unmarried daughter, or his eldest son's wife.

(c) Levying war against the King in his realm.

---

[1] Lord Hewart, C.J., in *Thomas* v. *Sawkins*, [1935] All E.R. Rep.655, 657; [1935] 2 K.B. 249, 254, *supra*, said: 'I think that there is quite sufficient ground for the proposition that it is part of the preventive power and, therefore, part of the preventive duty, of the police, in cases where there are such reasonable grounds of apprehension as the justices have found here, to enter and remain on private premises . . ." See also *Piddington* v. *Bates*, [1960] 3 All E.R.660; [1961] 1 W.L.R.162 (an appeal to the Divisional Court from conviction for obstruction of police officers in execution of their duty).

(d) Adhering to the King's enemies in the realm, giving them aid and comfort in the realm or outside. It has been held that the offence is committed whether the adherence is within or without the realm.[1]

(e) Slaying the Chancellor, Treasurer or the King's Justices, while in the discharge of their offices.

Two further types of treason added by later statutes are:

(f) Attempting to hinder the succession to the throne of any person entitled to succeed under the Act of Settlement, 1701.

(g) Maintaining in writing the invalidity of the line of succession established by the Act of Settlement.

Treason is punishable by death, and any prosecution for treason must be initiated within three years of the commission of the offence.

(2) *Sedition*

A seditious intention is an intention to bring into hatred or contempt, or to excite disaffection against, the Monarch in person, or the Government and Constitution of the United Kingdom as established by law, or either House of Parliament or the administration of justice, or to excite subjects of the Crown to attempt, otherwise than by lawful means, the alteration of any matter in Church or state by law established, or to raise discontent or disaffection among subjects of the Crown, or to promote feelings of ill-will and hostility between different classes of such subjects. So runs the description given of it by Cave J. in 1886.[2] Prosecutions for sedition are now rare, and are not normally instituted unless incitement to violence has taken place, but the term "sedition" may cover any of three common law offences:

(a) Publication of a seditious libel, that is, publication in a permanent form of matter of a seditious nature.

(b) Uttering of seditious words.

---

[1] *R. v. Lynch*, [1903] 1 K.B.444, where a British subject became a naturalised subject of the Boer Republic during the Boer War, and fought against the British. See also *R. v. Casement*, [1917] 1 K.B.98, where another British subject, during the 1914–1918 War, incited British prisoners of war in Germany to join the enemy forces and take part in an expedition against the British in Ireland; and *Joyce* v. *Director of Public Prosecutions*, [1946] 1 All E.R. 186; [1946] A.C.347, discussed below.

[2] *R. v. Burns* (1887), 16 Cox C.C.355.

(c) Conspiring to do an act in furtherance of a seditious intention.

(3) *Offences against the Official Secrets Acts*

Because the treasons listed as (c) and (d) above can only really be committed in war-time (the definition of an "enemy" being a citizen of a country with which the United Kingdom is at war), it has been found necessary to legislate with respect to offences of spying and sabotage[1] in peace-time. The Official Secrets Acts, 1911 and 1920, make it an offence, *inter alia*,

(a) to approach, inspect or enter any prohibited place, *i.e.*, an army or air force establishment, naval ship, arsenal etc.,

(b) to make sketches or plans which might be useful to an enemy,

(c) carelessly to part with such documents, or to retain them longer than permitted,

(d) to communicate documents or information to any person which might be useful to an enemy,

(e) to obstruct any of Her Majesty's forces in the vicinity of any prohibited place, or

(f) to wear an unauthorised uniform, to make a false declaration or to forge a passport or permit in order to gain admission to a prohibited place.

The width of these provisions has often been criticised, and in 1972 a Departmental Committee headed by Lord Franks recommended some modification of the law intended to ensure that prosecutions should be confined to cases where the alleged acts of the accused concern matters of real importance.

(4) *Miscellaneous offences*

A number of other offences against the state should be born in mind as of constitutional importance, but no attempt will be made here to explain or discuss them. The majority of them are statutory offences, and the list includes misprision of treason (concealment of the offence of treason), attempts to alarm or injure the Monarch,

---

[1] The use of prosecutions under the Official Secrets Acts in order to deal with acts of sabotage as well as spying was made clear by the House of Lords in *Chandler v. Director of Public Prosecutions*, [1962] 3 All E.R.142; [1964] A.C. 763.

incitement to mutiny or disaffection, trading with the enemy, and offences against the Foreign Enlistment Act, 1870.

Allegiance

In the case of treason and many of its kindred offences it is necessary before any prosecution can succeed that it should be proved that the accused owes allegiance to the Crown. The categories of persons who owe such allegiance are:

(a) British subjects,
(b) aliens resident in the United Kingdom, and
(c) aliens not resident in the United Kingdom, but who have previously been so resident, and have left either their families or their effects in the United Kingdom.

A short explanation of these three groups of persons is necessary.

(*a*) *British subjects.*—The attributes of British nationality are governed by a number of statutes, the most recent and important being the British Nationality Act, 1948, as amended by the British Nationality Acts, 1958, 1964 and 1965. The various methods of acquiring British nationality are complicated, but broadly speaking they are five-fold—birth, descent, naturalisation, registration and by incorporation of territory. But one of the most striking innovations brought about by the British Nationality Act, 1948, is the provision that all British subjects shall also possess citizenship *either* of the United Kingdom and colonies *or* of some other Commonwealth country. Commonwealth countries for this purpose are the independent members of the Commonwealth discussed in Chapter 13 below,[1] together with certain other countries which may not yet be fully independent, though independent in many respects, and which have been granted by the United Kingdom the privilege of possessing their own citizenship. It may be that a prime significance of this innovation in constitutional law is that, as far as the laws of the United Kingdom are concerned, only British subjects who are also citizens of the United Kingdom and colonies are now capable of committing treason by any act outside the United Kingdom and colonies, though there is as yet no case authority for this

---

[1] The republics within the Commonwealth, which will also be discussed in Chapter 13, have tended to abolish British nationality as regards their own citizens.

assertion. It is submitted that it is more accurate today to consider that for the purpose of the law of treason only this smaller group of British subjects owes permanent allegiance to the Crown, although in the more general law of the Commonwealth as a whole, discussed in Chapter 13, all British subjects owe allegiance to the Crown.

(b) and (c) *Aliens who owe temporary allegiance*.—In view of what has just been said, British subjects who are citizens of other Commonwealth countries may be regarded as coming into the same category as aliens for the purposes of allegiance to the criminal laws of the United Kingdom, though not for other purposes. The citizens of the Republic of Ireland, which is not a country within the Commonwealth at all, possess certain privileges under the terms of the Ireland Act, 1949, and they are not for other purposes regarded as aliens, but again they come into the same category as aliens as far as the law of treason is concerned. The same applies to British protected persons, who are generally speaking the inhabitants of British protectorates, and who also have a special status. Bearing this in mind, no explanation of the description "aliens resident in the United Kingdom" is required here. But non-resident aliens under group (c) above need some attention. The authority for the existence of the group is a resolution of the English judges in 1707[1] to the effect that any alien who had once resided in Great Britain,[2] and who had then departed from the country, but leaving his family or estate behind him, could still be dealt with as a traitor if he should transgress the law of treason—provided he returned or was brought back within the jurisdiction of the courts, for the trial of an absent man for treason would be abortive. The meaning of this resolution seems plain, but it has probably been rather broadened in scope as a result of the case of *Joyce* v. *Director of Public Prosecutions* in 1946.[3] In that case William Joyce, nicknamed "Lord Haw-Haw" in the United Kingdom, was tried and convicted for treason on the ground that he had broadcast for and adhered to the German cause, while living in Germany during the Second World War. The commission of the treasonable act was beyond doubt, but the

---

[1] Foster, *Crown Law*, p. 183.
[2] It will be recalled that the United Kingdom (then of Great Britain and Ireland) did not come into being until 1800: see Chapter 7, *ante*.
[3] [1946] All E.R.186; [1946] A.C.347.

accused was in fact a citizen of the United States of America. Nevertheless the jurisdiction of the English courts was held to be valid because he had obtained a British passport by false representations, and had renewed it shortly before the outbreak of war. Yet he had left no family or belongings of any kind in this country, and the passport was not even found in his possession. The House of Lords came to its decision by a majority, Lords SIMONDS, MACMILLAN and WRIGHT concurring with the speech of Lord JOWITT L.C., while only Lord PORTER dissented on the ground that the question whether Joyce was making use of his passport at the time of his broadcasts had not been drawn to the attention of the jury. Thus the principle in the judges' resolution of 1707 would seem to have been extended, and the decision is of the binding authority of the House of Lords, even though it has not infrequently been criticised. It is perhaps possible to suggest one reason for the decision which was not considered significant by the courts, namely that England was the *locus* of the crime, for although the treasonable acts were committed in Germany they would have had little point unless they were actually heard by listeners to the wireless broadcasts in England.

Apart from the law of treason and of certain other offences against the state, an alien in the United Kingdom enjoys full civic rights, provided his own country is at peace with the United Kingdom, although he may not own or have a share in a British ship or aircraft, nor may he vote or stand as a candidate in Parliamentary or local elections. The Crown may probably exclude aliens from the country whenever it wishes, under its Prerogative right, but in fact this is usually done, where necessary, by statutory provisions. Powers of internment and deportation are usually provided for by Act of Parliament. Enemy aliens can be arrested and imprisoned at common law, and they have no right to apply for a writ of habeas corpus against the Crown, or to bring civil actions, although they are permitted to defend civil actions or criminal prosecutions against them, and to appeal against adverse decisions of trial courts. There is legislation to control immigration to the United Kingdom from other parts of the Commonwealth, and to provide for deportation in certain cases. These provisions were considerably strengthened by the Immigration Act, 1971, but the law is in fact similar to that enforced by many Commonwealth countries.

Powers of extradition are provided for by reciprocal treaties with various countries, whereby the United Kingdom Government generally agrees (the exact agreement depends on the terms of each treaty) to hand over to such states any persons, whether British or not, either accused of or found guilty of committing any offences covered by the Extradition Acts, 1870–1935. These Acts cover most criminal offences, except those which are of a political nature. Thus no extradition will be allowed where the case is really one of an individual claiming political asylum.[1] Again, no extradition will be allowed where the accused has already been tried in the United Kingdom for the offence. The Fugitive Offenders Act, 1967 similarly provides for the arrest and surrender of persons who are accused of having committed crimes in other Commonwealth countries, and who have fled to the United Kingdom.

II. Duties of the Citizen in the United Kingdom

In the main body of this chapter the limitations upon the fundamental freedoms of the individual have been sketched. It is unnecessary to consider in any detail the constitutional duties of such individuals, because it can be appreciated that wherever the law has provided for a restriction upon full liberty it is the duty of all persons to obey that law. Similarly in respect of such freedom as remains after the restrictions upon it have been conceded, it is the duty of all persons to respect the individual liberties of others. Thus, to sum up, the laws of the United Kingdom provide for negative restrictions upon and safeguards for the constitutional rights of the individual. Such residuary rights must be respected by all persons, and can normally only be altered by Act of Parliament.[2] There is at once a privilege to enjoy these rights, and a complementary duty to respect them and to obey the law.

Further Reading

Clive Parry, *Nationality and Citizenship Laws of the Commonwealth and of the Republic of Ireland* (2 Vols., 1957 and 1960).

---

[1] As in *R.* v. *Governor of Brixton Prison, ex parte Kolczynski*, [1955] 1 All E.R.31; [1955] 1 Q.B.540.

[2] Two other possible, though rarer, methods are delegated legislation (see Chapter 10, *post*) and judicial decisions. As regards the latter method it is arguable that courts only develop, rather than change, the law. This is perhaps a question of interpretation: see *ante*, *Elias* v. *Pasmore*, [1934] 2 K.B.164, [1943] All E.R. Rep.380; and *Thomas* v. *Sawkins*, [1935] 2 K.B.249. [1935] All E.R. Rep.655.

Lord Denning, *Freedom under the Law* (1949), Chapter 2.
K. C. Wheare, *Modern Constitutions* (2nd ed., 1966).
Roscoe Pound, *The Development of Constitutional Guarantees of Liberty* (1957).
I. Brownlie, *Law Relating to Public Order* (1968).
H. Street, *Freedom, the Individual and the Law* (3rd ed., 1972).
D. Williams, *Not in the Public Interest* (1965).
D. Williams, *Keeping the Peace* (1967).

CHAPTER 9

THE CHURCH

Complete religious toleration is practised throughout the United Kingdom and the British Isles, and citizens are free to join or support any religious sect they wish. The sole limitation upon the scope given to all religious bodies is that provided by the criminal law of the land. For example, although members of certain Eastern religions are permitted by their faith to practise polygamy, the contraction of a polygamous marriage in the British Isles amounts to the crime of bigamy; and it is no defence to such a charge that any second ceremony of marriage was performed according to bona fide religious beliefs.

Of the many churches which maintain a following in the British Isles, however, two occupy a certain more privileged position than others, namely the Church of England (Episcopalian) and the Church of Scotland (Presbyterian). These two churches are said to be "established" churches, although this is not really a technical term and it does not imply that any other religious bodies, whether christian or not, are in any way discouraged. In particular the Roman Catholic Church has many adherents, whilst several non-conformist churches, notably the Methodist, Baptist and English United Reformed Churches, have widespread national organisations, as has also the Episcopalian or Anglican Church in Scotland. Again, there are many adherents to the Jewish faith in the United Kingdom. The Church of Ireland (Anglican) was "disestablished" in 1869 by the Irish Church Act, as was also the Church of England in Wales by the Welsh Church Act, 1914, and thus they occupy a similar position in the eyes of the law to all other non-privileged religious bodies in the British Isles. It will be recalled from Chapter 2, however, that priests of the Roman Catholic Church and clergy of the Church of Ireland are barred from membership of the House of Commons, as are also clergy of the Church of England and ministers of the Church of Scotland.

The effect of "establishment" differs slightly in each of the cases of the two churches concerned, and it is perhaps best to examine them separately.

I. THE CHURCH OF ENGLAND

The modern position of the protestant Church of England dates from the reign of Queen Elizabeth I, and in particular from the Act of Supremacy, 1558, and the Act of Uniformity, 1558, and its status was ratified in the Act of Union, 1707. In a sense the Church was recognised by the state as being that which in its opinion truly taught the christian faith. As has been mentioned in Chapter 3, the Monarch must be in communion with the Church of England,[1] and the Monarch's accession declaration and coronation oath, and the whole form of the coronation ceremony, and on certain other ceremonial occasions, is according to the beliefs of the Church of England. Archbishops and Bishops of the Church sit in the House of Lords,[2] whereas no other church is officially so represented, although any priest or minister of the Church of England or of any other church who is also a peer may of course sit in the Lords. But perhaps the greatest effect of establishment has been that the decrees of the Church are of legal authority throughout England. Its legislative body is now the General Synod, instituted by the Synodical Government Measure, 1969, and consisting of Bishops, clergy and laity. Any enactment which the Synod has decided to sponsor is formulated as a "Measure", which is then submitted to Parliament for approval, such approval, if obtained, being given by simple affirmative resolution of each House of Parliament. Once a Measure has passed Parliament it takes effect as if it were an Act of Parliament, but it applies directly only to the Church of England, and will affect other persons or bodies only negatively or indirectly. The work of the General Synod is assisted by 43 diocesan synods.

The executive organisation of the Church is according to a hierarchy, with Archbishops and Bishops as the superior authorities, priests and deacons as the lower orders, and with the Monarch as "Supreme Governor", though with no spiritual

---

[1] Bill of Rights, 1689, Coronation Oath Act, 1689, and Act of Settlement 1701.
[2] See Chapter 2, *ante.*

jurisdiction.[1] Many priests and deacons will, however, occupy posts of special ecclesiastical significance within a Bishop's diocese or within a local parish. Ecclesiastical courts of the Church of England are no longer of such general legal importance as they used to be before the middle of the nineteenth century, when they had competence in such matters as testamentary succession and matrimonial causes. Nowadays they have jurisdiction over internal ecclesiastical law only, usually concerning the interpretation of doctrine or the particular clerical behaviour of a clergyman. The hierarchy, composition and procedure of these courts was modernised by the Ecclesiastical Jurisdiction Measure, 1963 (1963 No. 1), but a final appeal in all matters still lies to the Judicial Committee of the Privy Council.

II. The Church of Scotland

The Church of Scotland is a protestant church, but with a non-episcopalian form of government. It received recognition in Scotland by a series of Acts of the Scottish Parliament before the union with England, and in the Treaty of Union, 1707, and the ratifying statutes of the two Parliaments, the establishment of both the Church of England and the Church of Scotland was guaranteed permanently for the future, although, as we have pointed out in Chapter 2, Parliament cannot bind itself absolutely for the future as far as statutes affecting England are concerned: as we have seen, the position may be different in Scotland. The special constitutional position of the Church of Scotland does not conflict with the status of the Church of England, for the latter is established within England only. Whereas the Church of England has as its "Supreme Governor" the Monarch, who is also temporal head of the state, the Church of Scotland claims to exercise unfettered spiritual sovereignty, and thus to possess a jurisdiction *jure divino* coordinate with that of the state. The legislative Acts of its General Assembly are regarded as statutes of the realm, needing neither Parliamentary approval nor the Royal Assent.

The organisation of the clergy of the Church of Scotland is not founded upon an hierarchical system, and thus there are no Bishops or other superior clergymen of the Church. The Church

---

[1] Act of Supremacy, 1558.

is governed by a hierarchy of courts, Kirk Session, Presbytery, Synod and General Assembly, in all of which ordained clergymen, called ministers, and lay elders have equal place. Each is presided over by a clerical Moderator, and the Moderator of the General Assembly ranks as the leader of the Church during his year of office. Although the Monarch is not the "Supreme Governor" of the Church, he or his Commissioner has the right to attend sessions of the General Assembly of the Church,[1] and it is conventional for him to attend services of the Church of Scotland when in Scotland. The Church courts enforce church discipline etc. in much the same way as in the Church of England. The Church is entitled to legislate for itself, and does so normally through resolutions of its General Assembly,[2] which, as has been pointed out above, do not require the approval of Parliament. It is perhaps for this reason that there is no direct representation of the Church in the House of Lords, as there is in the case of the Church of England.

It may therefore be seen that both the Church of England and the Church of Scotland maintain privileged positions in the constitutional system of the United Kingdom, but in effect their authority as established churches is restricted to England and Scotland respectively, and all churches are really of equal status in Wales and Northern Ireland.

FURTHER READING

Sir Thomas Taylor, "Church and State in Scotland", [1957] *Juridicial Review* 121.

R. King Murray, "The Constitutional Position of the Church of Scotland", [1958] *Public Law* 155.

Sir H. W. Cripps, *A Practical Treatise on the Law Relating to the Church and Clergy*, (8th ed., by K. M. Macmorran, 1937).

E. Garth Moore, *An Introduction to English Canon Law* (1967).

---

[1] Act 1592, cap. 8, of the Scottish Parliament (often referred to as "the Charter of the Church"), which is still in force.
[2] Church of Scotland Act, 1921.

PART II

PRINCIPLES OF
ENGLISH ADMINISTRATIVE LAW

INTRODUCTION

In the second part of this book we are only concerned with English law, rather than the general law of the United Kingdom This is because, unlike other parts of constitutional law, administrative law has been built up in each of the component countries of the union as a separate and individual entity. No direct and apposite comparison can be made between the administrative laws of England and Scotland or Northern Ireland although it is true to say once more that the law of Northern Ireland is not greatly dissimilar from that of England.

The term "administrative law" is difficult to define, for the scope of its subject has become very wide in recent years, and there is every indication that it will become even wider in the future. It may, however, be stated generally that it amounts to the law concerning the administration. This might have been a simple concept if it were not that the powers and sphere of influence of the administration in the United Kingdom today have spread so greatly to embrace almost every aspect of everyday life in the modern state.[1] Perhaps it is best to describe administrative law as that law which is concerned with any aspects of the administration of the country, and in particular the law governing the relationship between the state and the individual. In this latter respect it is inextricably bound up with the general law concerning civil actions, and it is for this reason above all that the administrative laws of the countries of the United Kingdom differ, for their general municipal laws have grown up separately.[2] It is

---

[1] See Chapter 3, *ante.*
[2] See Chapter 1, *ante.*

submitted that English administrative law is of more widespread importance than the administrative laws of Scotland or Northern Ireland, for the administrative laws throughout the Commonwealth are based upon it far more than upon the administrative laws of other countries in the union, and in any case the law of Northern Ireland in many ways reflects it. Scots administrative law is really the "odd man out", and, as in numerous respects it defies comparison with the principles of the English law, particularly for example on the subject of remedies of the individual against the administration, which are quite distinct and cover different circumstances in Scotland from those in England, it is not intended here to indulge in any comparison of the two systems. This part of the book will be confined to English administrative law.

CHAPTER 10

SUBORDINATE LEGISLATION

It has been seen in Chapter 2 that in the United Kingdom the power to legislate is vested in Parliament at Westminster.[1] This power is supplemented by the adjudicatory function of the law courts, which apply and interpret Acts of Parliament as may be necessary, but which also follow the rules established by the method of case precedent wherever no statute law is relevant.[2] But there is still another method of law-making, known as delegated or subordinate legislation, which stems from the position of Parliament as a sovereign body, even though it is not a manifestation of the direct functioning of Parliament. Wherever an Act of Parliament provides that any Government Department, local authority, the Crown, or any individual or body shall have the power to make regulations or orders that shall have the force of law, that statute is regarded as laying down a method of creating delegated legislation, and any regulations or orders made under such powers take effect as if part of the "parent" Act,[3] provided that they conform to the limitations expressed in that parent Act.[4] The power to legislate in this way may, however, be conferred only by an Act of Parliament, or, more rarely, by the Royal Prerogative. The term "subordinate legislation" really includes law-making under the power of the Royal Prerogative, discussed above in Chapter 3, as where the Crown legislates by Proclamation or Order in Council for newly conquered or ceded colonies. But *delegated* legislation, properly so called, may only be created under statutory powers, and it is this subject which it is our main purpose to consider in the present chapter. Nevertheless, whether

---

[1] But note the special subordinate position of the Northern Ireland Assembly, discussed in Chapter 7, *ante.*
[2] See Chapter 4, *ante.*
[3] *Institute of Patent Agents* v. *Lockwood*, [1894] A.C.347.
[4] *Minister of Health* v. *R., ex parte Yaffe*, [1931] A.C.494; [1931] All E.R. Rep.343.

the authority for subordinate legislation be, in any particular instance, a statute or the Royal Prerogative, the person or body empowered to create the subordinate legislation is usually a part of the Crown, as we shall see presently, and thus the law concerning the effect and control of this legislation is administrative law. It may also be noted in passing that, in the case of delegated legislation, the parent Act may provide for sub-delegation of powers conferred, but that sub-delegation is only lawful if authorised expressly or by necessary implication by the enabling Act.

The necessity for the existence of subordinate legislation is primarily dictated by the exigencies of modern life in a democratic community. An enormous amount of regulation is required to ensure orderly and just provision for the needs of all citizens. There is far too much for Parliament alone to deal with in detail, and in any case some regulations have to be brought into force at very short notice in view of sudden changes of, for example, economic conditions. Parliament would be unlikely to be able to pass a Bill to meet such conditions sufficiently quickly, as its immediate programme of business may already be full. Again, the need for certain new regulations is often appreciated by Government Departments, which have special means of knowing the conditions prevailing in the country or the world in its own field of interest, but may not be apparent to M.P.s who are not members of the Government or of that Department, and who may belong to an opposition party which would feel bound to oppose the measure for political reasons, as in the case of a Bill before the House. It has therefore become increasingly recognised by responsible persons during the past half-century that discretionary powers must be vested by Parliament in specific persons or bodies, though in most cases with careful safeguards to prevent abuse of such power. Although Lord Hewart severely criticised the growth of delegated legislation in his book *The New Despotism*, published in 1929 while the author was still in office as Lord Chief Justice of England, the fears that had prompted the publication were soothed by the later *Report of the Committee on Ministers' Powers* in 1932.[1] The result of this Report was that consistent opposition to the existence of the powers became less frequent. and the energies of those who had previously felt their danger

---

[1] Cmd.4060.

were directed into reinforcing the safeguards surrounding the exercise of such powers.

Types of delegated legislation

In effect it is open to Parliament to create any delegated legislative power it wishes, in whatever form and vested in whatever person or body it cares, for this is a power implicit in the sovereignty of Parliament. For example, it has sometimes conferred a power to impose taxation, or even to modify or adapt the parent Act or other Acts of Parliament, though Parliament will not normally do this without good reason. The most usual types of delegated legislation which have been provided for by statute in the past can be tabulated without great difficulty, and there is no reason to believe that Parliament will wish in the future to depart from its established practice. The main varieties are:

(1) Local authority bye-laws. Thus in statutes creating local authorities or in any way altering the powers of such authorities that already exist it is common to include a section or sections empowering the authorities to make local bye-laws or regulations which shall have effect as binding law upon the persons in the district. An account of the system of local government will be seen in Chapter 12 below.

(2) Public corporation bye-laws. The nature of public corporations has already been described in Chapter 3, and the power of these corporations to make bye-laws for the regulation of their business, employees etc. is similarly frequently included in statutes creating them or altering their powers.

(3) Rules of the Supreme Court and of the County Court etc. Rules committees are sometimes set up by statute specifically empowered to make rules concerning the practice and procedure of the courts already described in Chapter 4.

(4) Regulations made by the European Commission, subject to prior approval of the Council of Ministers.

(5) Ministerial or Departmental regulations. These, together with the delegated legislation in category (6) below, are the most common and widely used of delegated legislative powers, and they are called statutory instruments. This is why delegated legislation falls under the heading of

administrative law, even though in theory such a power to
create legislation may be conferred by Parliament upon
anyone, and not just upon the administration.

(6) Orders made by the Monarch in Council. These are often
similar in nature to Ministerial or Departmental regulations,
but they are generally of wider national importance, and the
authority for their creation may stem from the Royal
Prerogative as well as from Parliament. Instead of being
formulated entirely by the Minister or Government
Department primarily concerned, without any outside
help or advice being necessary, they may originate as the
embodiment of Government policy, but must receive the
assent of the Monarch in the Privy Council before they may
come into effect. In practice the distinction between Orders
in Council and Ministerial or Departmental regulations is
perhaps not vital, because a normal meeting of the Privy
Council will consist of the Monarch, three or four Ministers
who are Privy Councillors, including the Lord President of
the Council, and the Clerk to the Privy Council, but the
procedure does at least ensure slightly more publicity and the
possibility of second thoughts on the part of the Government.

It will be realised that in the case of the last two types of
delegated legislation any powers which are conferred by statute
will enable the Government of the day to enforce its policy
decisions as being law, which could result in a grave abuse of the
trust imposed in the executive. But the responsibility of Ministers
to Parliament is an important check on any such tendency, even
though it would probably be possible for the Government to
force any Bill embodying its desires through Parliament by means
of its party majority if it really wished. The executive control of,
or at least predominance of power in, Parliament would lead to
the same policy becoming law, but the advantages of delegated
legislation from the point of view of the Government are those of
speed, especially in emergencies or in war-time, the ability to
deal with a technical subject-matter without having to explain
the whole issue painstakingly to Parliament, and flexibility, in
that regulations may be made, altered or rescinded as and when it
is thought appropriate and without unnecessary delay. To set
against these advantages it may be urged that the lack of general
publicity consequent upon dealing with such matters in the

ordinary legislative form in Parliament may be harmful and unfair, but certain safeguards have been brought into being to counteract any such undesirable trends.

A. *Parliamentary Safeguards*

(1) *Laying before Parliament*

In order to provide that Parliament shall at least have cognisance of such delegated legislation as is of national importance, namely Orders in Council and Ministerial and Departmental regulations, the enabling Act very often now provides that any regulations made under the terms of the Act, or any draft Orders in Council which are proposed, shall be laid before Parliament or before one or other of the Houses of Parliament.[1] It seems likely that Parliament will in due course extend the laying procedure in some form to regulations made by the European Commission, and that subsequent scrutiny of such regulations may be exercised by a Joint Committee of both Houses of Parliament. In many cases there is no express power vested in the House or Houses by the enabling Act to vote on the matter, and thus the "laying before" is purely for the information of members; and in some cases indeed the delegated legislation may already have come into force. Members may, however, ask Parliamentary questions concerning the instrument, even though it is not possible for the House to vote on the matter directly. On the other hand it is sometimes provided that the regulation shall not come into force or continue in force unless an affirmative resolution of one or both of the Houses shall have been passed, or else that the regulation or order shall become or remain law unless one or other House annuls it by a negative vote within a specific time. It must be emphasised that the specific kinds of "laying before" under the principle discussed here may theoretically be limitless in number, because in each case the nature of the control depends upon the terms of the parent Act. But the Report of the Select Committee on Delegated Legislation in 1953 declares that there are only three types of "laying before" in practice, namely those already mentioned:

(a) the laying of an instrument before either or both of the

---

[1] To the author's knowledge there has never yet been a statutory provision that an instrument should be laid before the House of Lords only, but in principle there is no reason why such a provision should not be enacted.

Houses for information, Parliament having no power under the terms of the parent Act to vote on the instrument;

(b) the laying of an instrument before either or both of the Houses, with the requirement of an affirmative resolution to bring it into force or to continue it in force; and

(c) the laying of an instrument before either or both of the Houses, with the possibility (but no requirement) of a negative vote which would annul it or prevent it coming into force.

(2) *The Scrutiny Committees*

In the House of Commons there is a Select Committee on Statutory Instruments, set up in 1944 as a delayed implementation of one of the recommendations of the Committee on Ministers' Powers.[1] "Statutory instruments" is a collective term which covers all Orders in Council made under statutory powers (as opposed to those made under the Prerogative power), together with such Ministerial or Departmental regulations as may be designated statutory instruments by their enabling Acts, but not other varieties of delegated legislation. The Committee is empowered to scrutinise all statutory instruments which are laid before the House, and as regards which the House has the power, under the particular enabling Act, to take any action, *i.e.* by either affirmative or negative resolution. Thus all instruments laid before the House which fall under headings (b) or (c) above, but not those under (a), are referred to the Committee. It is not proper for the Committee to comment upon the policy of any instrument, but it has the duty to draw the attention of the House to any instrument which needs elucidation, or which purports to make unexpected or unusual use of the powers conferred in the parent Act, because it purports to exclude the possibility of challenge in the courts, or for similar reasons concerning form only. It is perhaps a tribute to Departmental integrity and conscientiousness that the Committee has only found it necessary to draw the attention of the House to a few out of the total number of instruments referred to it.

A somewhat similar Committee, the Special Orders Committee, has existed in the Lords since 1925, but its power is rather more

---

[1] Cmd.4060 (1932), pp. 67–69.

limited in that it may only scrutinise and report upon those instruments which require an affirmative resolution of the House before coming into effect or continuing in force, *i.e.* instruments laid before the House which fall under heading (b) above, but not those falling under (a) or (c).

(3) *Other Parliamentary safeguards*

Additional Parliamentary safeguards are inherent in the power of members of either House to ask questions concerning, *inter alia*, delegated legislation, to call for a debate (probably through the Leader of the Opposition), and even in extreme cases to move the censure of the Government. Such procedures may be particularly useful in respect of delegated legislation in the form of statutory instruments which only have to be laid before Parliament, or one of the Houses of Parliament, for information, and where consequently there is no possibility of a direct affirmative or negative resolution, *i.e.* instruments falling under heading (a) above.

B. *Judicial Safeguards*

If any delegated legislation, of whatever kind, is formulated contrary to the terms of its enabling Act, or in excess of the powers conferred, then it may be challenged in the courts as being *ultra vires* the enabling Act. The actual methods whereby such challenge may be pursued will be considered in the next chapter, but for the present it is sufficient to say that although delegated legislation takes effect as if it is part of its parent Act,[1] and is thus of statutory force, yet this result does not come about unless the delegated legislation in *intra vires*, that is, properly formulated according to the terms of the Act.[2] Although Acts of Parliament are immune from judicial challenge, delegated legislation can be challenged in the courts on the ground that it is *ultra vires*, and this may include the power of the courts to hold delegated legislation bad as being unreasonable.[3]

---

[1] *Institute of Patent Agents* v. *Lockwood*, [1894] A.C.347.
[2] *Minister of Health* v. *R.*, *ex parte Yaffe*, [1931] A.C.494; [1931] All E.R. Rep.343; *R.* v. *Halliday*, *ex parte Zadig*, [1917] A.C.260. See also *Allingham* v. *Minister of Agriculture*, [1948] 1 All E.R.780, where an invalid sub-delegation of power had been made.
[3] See, *e.g.*, *Kruse* v. *Johnson*, [1898] 2 Q.B.91.

C. *Political Safeguards*

It may sometimes be provided in the parent Act that the Minister concerned should consult interested bodies or an Advisory Committee before issuing regulations. Again, the Statutory Instruments Act, 1946, provides that all statutory instruments shall be published by the Stationery Office after they have been made. Where any statutory instrument is required to be laid before Parliament after being made, the published copies must contain the date on which it came or will come into operation. Such provisions are useful in ensuring a reasonable amount of consultation before committing a policy to become law, and in making provision for any interested party to be able to read the terms of the instrument concerned, but they are perhaps not strictly methods of control. But any person charged with an offence under a statutory instrument has a good defence if he can prove that the instrument had not at the time of the offence been published by the Stationery Office, unless reasonable steps had been taken to bring the instrument to the notice of the public, the person charged or persons likely to be affected by it.[1]

It is possible that some additional method ought to be devised to bring instruments to the notice of the general public more readily than by publications of the Stationery Office, although it may be unrealistic to imagine that an apathetic populace would avail itself of such wider publicity. The present provision for publication of statutory instruments does at least provide for *some* publicity of the measures concerned, and thus it may facilitate one final safeguard against unwarranted acts of the executive, namely that of public opinion. Great unpopularity may make it politically expedient for the Government to change its policy and to rescind any regulations already made.[2] This is essentially a topic outside the scope of a lawyer, but it is possible that such a political safeguard is a real supplement to the existing legal safeguards, and that it ensures that the legitimate purposes of delegated legislation are not misused to any serious extent.

---

[1] Statutory Instruments Act, 1946, s.3(2).
[2] An instance of the effect of public opinion (although not a case of delegated legislation) was the agitation leading to the setting up of a Public Inquiry into the Crichel Down affair in 1954: see *Public Inquiry ordered by the Minister of Agriculture into the disposal of land at Crichel Down*, Cmd. 9176 (1954).

FURTHER READING

H. W. R. Wade, *Administrative Law* (3rd ed., 1971).

J. F. Garner, *Administrative Law* (3rd ed., 1970).

D. C. M. Yardley, *A Source Book of English Administrative Law* (2nd ed., 1970).

Sir Carleton K. Allen, *Law and Orders* (3rd ed., 1965).

J. A. G. Griffith and H. Street, *Principles of Administrative Law* (4th ed., 1967).

M. A. Sieghart, *Government by Decree* (1950).

D. Foulkes, *Introduction to Administrative Law* (3rd ed., 1972).

G. J. Borrie, *Public Law* (2nd ed., 1970).

CHAPTER 11

TRIBUNALS, INQUIRIES AND THE CONTROL
OF POWER

Administrative law, as has been said at the beginning of Part II of this book, is a special sub-division of constitutional law, and there has been an increasing tendency in this century for it to be made to cover a number of topics and problems which fall outside the ordinary scope of the common law courts. It is for this reason that many so-called administrative tribunals have been set up to deal with such subjects. Departmental inquiries may also take place before an administrative decision is made. In the previous chapter we have seen how the administration frequently has subordinate legislative powers conferred upon it. But administrative law is also concerned with executive and judicial powers of the administration. We have already described in Chapter 3 how the Crown exercises its executive functions directly, and it is now our task to consider the tribunals and authorities which have been set up for the purpose of dealing with various aspects of administrative law, and which have either executive or judicial functions, and sometimes a mixture of the two. The Crown is the embodiment of the administration as a whole, but its function is not ended there: it is a subordinate legislature, acting under powers conferred by Act of Parliament or by the Royal Prerogative, and it also exercises judicial powers, as conferred upon it from time to time by Parliament. Yet there is a clear division between the position of administrative authorities, other than the Crown direct, acting in executive or judicial capacities and other authorities acting as subordinate legislatures, for executive and judicial powers are often conferred upon tribunals separate from the Crown, even if appointed by the Crown whereas only the Crown itself or some part of it has ever had the power to exercise all three functions conferred upon it by Parliament. It is for this reason that subordinate legislation ha been considered separately in the last chapter, while the powers of tribunals, other than the Crown, are considered here. We shall examine first administrative tribunals, then inquiries, and finally the methods of control by the ordinary courts of law both of tribunals and of the Crown and other administrative authorities.

I. ADMINISTRATIVE TRIBUNALS

All administrative tribunals are set up by Act of Parliament or under powers conferred by statute, and their composition depends upon the statutory terms governing them. It would probably be more accurate to designate them "statutory tribunals", since their powers are mainly judicial rather than administrative, but the traditional term is now so well established that the use of any different description would only serve to confuse. It may be asked why there is any need for such tribunals, since pure administration can normally be carried out by the Crown or its servants, and judicial decisions can be obtained through the ordinary courts of law. The answer to this question is that there are nowadays too many problems of law and administration for the courts to cope with effectively, and the pure administrative functions of these tribunals are really subsidiary to their judicial functions. The number of cases involving these problems is enormous, and the requirements in dealing with such problems are mainly speed, cheapness, a special aptitude for the particular type of problems concerned (a quality provided for by the composition of each tribunal), lack of formality and forms, and in most cases the provision of rough and ready justice. Tribunals of various kinds are far more readily adapted to these needs than are the ordinary courts, and thus for the most part are able to perform their tasks to the greatest advantage of the various parties concerned. Many of the existing tribunals have in the past been severely criticised, largely, it is submitted, because of the previously widespread practice of not publishing their decisions or giving reasons for their decisions, and also partly in ignorance of the valuable work which is done by tribunals with little or no fuss or publicity. It is, however, true to say that certain tribunals have on occasions committed serious errors either of law or judgment, and these have received publicity. Criticism of administrative tribunals was among the reasons leading to the setting up of a Committee on

Administrative Tribunals and Enquiries, under the chairmanship of Sir Oliver Franks, which reported in July 1957.[1] The majority of the recommedations of this Committee were accepted by the major political parties, many were implemented by Government Departments as matters of policy, and a Tribunals and Inquiries Act, 1958, was passed to provide for the enactment of such of the recommendations as required immediate statutory effect. This statute, together with certain amendments and additions, has now been re-enacted as the Tribunals and Inquiries Act, 1971.

Detailed criticisms of administrative tribunals have in the main been three-fold:

(*a*) That they are totally unnecessary. This criticism has probably been finally answered by the findings of the Franks Committee that they are absolutely necessary, and even desirable, in modern conditions,[2] though some methods of control should be strengthened. The Committee also emphasised that the three great principles which should always be followed by such tribunals were those of openness, fairness and impartiality. On the whole these principles have usually been observed in the past, and it is clear that they are carefully followed today.

(*b*) That a system of entirely separate administrative courts should be set up, rather like the French system of courts concerned only with the *droit administratif*, or alternatively that there should be set up an Administrative Appeal Court or an Administrative Division of the High Court, to hear appeals direct in all cases from administrative tribunals. The Franks Committee decided against these suggestions, but it did, as we shall see presently, recommend an extension of the possibilities of direct appeal. Despite the Franks Committee there remains a considerable body of opinion among English lawyers favouring at least the creation of an Administrative Division of the High Court.[3]

(*c*) That all administrative procedure should be standardised, as in the United States of America, where there is a federal American Administrative Procedure Act, passed in 1946.

---

[1] Cmd.218.
[2] Cmd.218 (1957), paras. 403, 406.
[3] See *e.g.*, *Administration under Law* (a Report by JUSTICE, 1971).

This Act has been only partly successful, because of the great diversity of work covered by administrative agencies, and the Franks Committee probably extracted the value from this criticism without adopting it *in toto*, by recommending the setting up of a Council on Tribunals to keep a watchful eye upon the procedure of the various tribunals, and to recommend changes where it thinks fit.

It is not usually necessary for a law student to have any detailed knowledge of the various types of tribunals, and fuller lists, including the detailed duties and powers of each tribunal, may be studied elsewhere.[1] In this book we are concerned only with principles, and it should be noted that tribunals may be of any kind at all. Whatever their composition or detailed powers they will be regarded as administrative tribunals provided that their functions in some way involve a consideration of the relationships of or disputes between the state and the individual.

Examples are the General Commissioners of Income Tax, the Lands Tribunal, Independent Schools Tribunals, Local Valuation Courts and Mental Health Review Tribunals. There are also some tribunals which are set up to deal with disputes which arise between individuals, and which are in fact of little or no interest to the state as such so far as their individual decisions are concerned. Examples would be Rent Tribunals and Rent Assessment Committees. In some foreign countries, such as France, it is very doubtful whether this latter group of tribunals would be considered as dealing with anything outside the realm of ordinary private law,[2] but they are still regarded as administrative tribunals in this country because they deal with subjects which are outside the scope of the common law courts, and which are an integral part of the broad social policy of the country. It is probably also correct to consider the Restrictive Practices Court, created by the Restrictive Trade Practices Act, 1956, as an administrative tribunal, even though it contains judges of the High Court (in addition to other non-lawyer members) who are not sitting by

---

[1] *E.g.* Sir Carleton K. Allen, *Administrative Jurisdiction* (1956), reprinted from [1956] *Public Law* 13; the Annual Reports of the Council on Tribunals; and D. C. M. Yardley, *A Source Book of English Administrative Law* (2nd ed., 1970), Chapter 6.

[2] See C. J. Hamson, *Executive Discretion and Judicial Control: an Aspect of the Conseil d'Etat* (1954).

virtue of their offices in the High Court, and who, when sitting, do not wear wigs or gowns. The Patents Appeal Tribunal has a somewhat similar composition, and, as its title shows, is actually designated a tribunal.

A number of matters concerning tribunals generally may be briefly noted:

(1) Following the Franks Committee recommendation, a Council on Tribunals now advises the Lord Chancellor and the Secretary of State for Scotland upon the general supervision and procedure of tribunals and inquiries, and makes reports to Parliament upon its work.

(2) Chairmen, and in certain other cases the members, of tribunals are normally selected by the appropriate Minister from a panel of persons appointed by the Lord Chancellor.

(3) Chairmen of tribunals generally have legal training.

(4) Legal representation is normally allowed, if required by any of the parties who appear before tribunals.

(5) There is a full disclosure of all material facts to all parties before a tribunal hearing, and adequate notice of such a hearing is given.

(6) Hearings are held in public, unless public security is involved or intimate personal or financial matters, or professional capacity or reputation, are concerned.

(7) Reasons for decisions must be given, if requested.

(8) The Franks Committee recommended that there should normally be an appellate tribunal to hear appeals on fact, law or the merits from any first instance tribunal, but that otherwise no special appeal tribunal or court should be set up. This particular recommendation has never yet been implemented. It is, however, submitted that it is hard to visualise any useful way in which appeals on *fact* can lie to an appellate tribunal without such an appeal developing into a simple re-hearing of the issue which was heard below. If that were to happen the tribunal hearings would be robbed of their virtues of speed and cheapness. From such an appellate tribunal, when constituted, the Committee recommended that there should be an appeal on law only to the Divisional Court (or the Court of Session in Scotland). Although the Tribunals and Inquiries Act did not institute appeals to an appellate tribunal,

it did provide for appeals on law to lie from most tribunals to the Divisional Court (or Court of Session). The effect of the enactment, therefore, is to provide for appeals on law to the court in the case of most of the tribunals from which such appeals did not already lie.[1]

(9) Appellate tribunals now usually publish selected decisions for the guidance of lower tribunals. It may be stated with some confidence that since the implementation of most of the Franks Committee's recommendations there is no longer any substantial reason for dissatisfaction with the powers and duties of tribunals.

II. INQUIRIES

Where Parliament has decided to entrust the power to make decisions concerning aspects of administrative law to some person or persons independent of the administration it will normally confer this power on a tribunal. But much decision-making affecting the administration is retained in the hands of Ministers and their Departments. It is, however, quite common for a statute to provide that a Minister may only make a decision after first following a procedure intended to enable those who will be affected by his decision to make their views known; and this procedure is called an inquiry. The most usual inquiries are concerned with proposals which affect private property rights, and so inquiry procedures are used, for example, in connection with schemes to create new towns, appeals to the Minister against refusal by a local planning authority of proposals to develop land, and proposals to acquire private land compulsorily for housing, or in order to build airports or new motorways. The inquiry is conducted by an inspector, who must be careful to allow all objectors a fair chance to put their case, and the inspector then makes a report and recommendations to the Minister.

The Franks Committee, which has already been referred to, was required to consider the system of both tribunals and inquiries, and a number of the reforms subsequently effected have concerned

---

[1] See *Rule of Law* (Conservative Political Centre, 1955), Appendix, in which are listed the most important tribunals from which appeals of various kinds, either to a court or to another tribunal or to the Minister, already lay before the Act.

the latter. (It is curious that the Committee was asked to deal with "Enquiries", whilst Parliament then legislated for "Inquiries"! The most far-reaching reform stems from the provision, now in the Tribunals and Inquiries Act, 1971, that the Lord Chancellor may make rules regulating the procedure to be followed where any inquiries are held on behalf of a Minister, and such rules have been made covering a number of the most common types of inquiry particularly those held before a Minister decides on the merits of appeals to him against local refusal of planning permission. These rules now specify the period of notice to be given before an inquiry is held, the procedure to be adopted at the inquiry the form of the inspector's report to the Minister, and the way in which the Minister's eventual decision, together with reasons must be notified to the parties concerned. In particular it is provided that where a Minister differs from the inspector on a finding of fact, or takes into account any new issue of fact, and is in consequence disposed to disagree with any recommendation made by the inspector, he must give the parties who appeared at the inquiry an opportunity of making representations or of having the inquiry reopened before he makes any decision contrary to the inspector's recommendations. It will be readily seen therefore, that Ministers are far less free than they were before the Franks Committee reported to make decisions in this field which pay scant regard to the weight of evidence at prior inquiries Perhaps the trend of greater control over the powers of Minister is in this area taken to its fullest extent by the provisions, in the Town and Country Planning Act, 1968, for the final determination by the inspector himself of a number of appeals against the refusal of planning permission. This effectively removes the decision making power from the Minister altogether, even though the provision was really made to relieve the Department of a flood of minor appeals.

III. JUDICIAL CONTROL: GROUNDS

In the previous chapter it was stated that a consideration of the detailed procedure for judicial control of delegated legislation would be deferred until the present chapter. It is now our task to explain the procedures which are used not only for the judicial control of delegated legislation, but also for the control by the courts of administrative tribunals, inquiries and various powers exercised by the Crown, and sometimes also for more general purposes in purely private law, a problem which does not concern us here. It is proposed first to describe briefly the grounds upon which judicial control may be exercised, and then to list and describe the actual remedies which are used.

The grounds for judicial control are basically three in number:

(1) That the jurisdiction of the tribunal or other administrative authority was defective. This is generally called the *ultra vires* doctrine, but there are many different ways in which it may be invoked. Thus an act may have been done by the wrong authority; or the authority may not have been properly appointed or constituted; or the authority may have exceeded its power; or some fact which is a condition precedent to the possession of power by an authority may have been absent; or power may have been exercised in bad faith, unreasonably, for an improper purpose, or after taking irrelevant considerations into account.

(2) That the authority acted in breach of natural justice. There are two distinct rules of natural justice, namely:

   (*a*) that each interested party must have been heard, after being properly acquainted with any case that has been made against him; and

   (*b*) that an authority must act in the absence of any reasonable suspicion that it was biased, or had any substantial personal, pecuniary or proprietary interest in a dispute before it.

(3) That the authority acted in error of law. Some errors of law committed by, say, a tribunal may well go to jurisdiction, but it is also possible to be in error of law while nevertheless acting properly within jurisdiction. As we shall see in the next section of this chapter, it is possible to sue the Crown directly in tort, and in such cases also it would seem that the essential basis of the suit is that the Crown has acted in error of law.

In recent years the courts have made it clear that anything done *ultra vires* or in breach of natural justice is void, while an error of law within jurisdiction merely renders whatever has been done voidable, and thus needing to be quashed. It used to be thought that judicial control of administrative authorities was only possible where they were under a duty to act judicially, but the

House of Lords decided in the important case of *Ridge* v. *Baldwin* in 1963[1] that the courts were free to examine any act by such an inferior authority, and to set it aside if one of the grounds for judicial review was established. In any event it has long been accepted that delegated legislation may be set aside if it should prove to be *ultra vires*.

IV. JUDICIAL CONTROL: THE REMEDIES

The actual remedies by which judicial control may be achieved may be divided into two main groups, those which are direct and those which are indirect.

A. *Direct Remedies*

The direct remedies in this field are primarily either appeals (provided by the statutes governing the various tribunals and other authorities) or actions for damages. But it should also be noted that a defence to a prosecution for an offence under delegated legislation may well take the form of an assertion that the regulation concerned is *ultra vires*. This, if successful, would be a particularly direct form of remedy.

It is not necessary to explain the nature of an appeal, and the identity of the courts or bodies to hear appeals from tribunals will depend upon the terms of the various statutes. But from most tribunals for which no appellate structure already existed the Tribunals and Inquiries Act, 1971, s. 13 (re-enacting a provision in the earlier 1958 Act), provides that an appeal on law lies direct to the High Court. Nor is it intended here to explain the elements of an action for damages which will lie wherever a tort has been committed or there has been a breach of contract. It is most unlikely that such an action would be appropriate against a tribunal not directly connected with the Crown, which can rarely be a party to a contract or commit a tort. It may well be possible however, that grounds for actions for damages may from time to time arise against Ministers (sometimes deciding matters after inquiries) or other servants of the Crown. Until the passage of the Crown Proceedings Act, 1947, actions in tort were not available against the Crown, and actions in contract could only be brought

---

[1] [1963] 2 All E.R.6 A66; [1964] A.C.40.

after a petition of right had been granted by the Crown itself, the petition having the effect of giving permission to the aggrieved person to bring his action. Some attention must therefore be accorded briefly to this statute and the resultant legal position.

The Crown Proceedings Act 1947

Section 1 provides in effect that any person or body may bring an action in contract direct against a Government Department, except in three types of case. The exceptions are cases in which the Crown remains privileged from legal actions for damages, or for the recovery of a liquidated sum, or for specific performance,[1] and cover contracts dependent upon a future grant of money from Parliament (for no litigant can be allowed to force Parliament to grant funds to enable the Government to carry out its contractual obligations), contracts which fetter future executive action,[2] and contracts of service with members of the armed forces.[3] Thus, to take an example from the last exception, no soldier has the right to sue the Crown for wrongful dismissal, or for reduction or arrears of pay. The reason for this is that the armed forces are still under the Prerogative power of the Crown, as has been seen in Chapter 3, except in so far as funds for their upkeep etc. must be provided annually by Parliament.

Section 2 provides that actions in tort may now be brought directly against Government Departments or against the Crown as a whole, although only in specific circumstances, namely:

  (1) in respect of torts committed by its servants or agents,
  (2) in respect of any breach of duties which a person owes to his servants or agents at common law by reason of being their employer,

---

[1] It will be seen presently that no injunction will lie against the Crown.

[2] It is not really clear what this phrase means. There are very few direct cases upon the point: see J. D. B. Mitchell, *The Contracts of Public Authorities* (1954); D. Foulkes, *Introduction to Administrative Law* (3rd ed., 1972), pp. 210–214; D. C. M. Yardley, *A Source Book of English Administrative Law* (2nd ed., 1970), Chapter 7.

[3] The position would seem now to be different in the case of contracts of service with civil servants. The Industrial Relations Act, 1971, s. 22, provides for a procedure before an Industrial Tribunal in cases of alleged unfair dismissal of employees. Crown servants, other than members of the armed forces, are not listed among the exclusions later made in the Act. But some doubt must remain because there is no section of the Act making it expressly binding on the Crown. And there is anyway still no provision for action to be taken by civil servants against the Crown in the courts.

(3) in respect of any breach of the duties attaching at common law to the ownership, occupation, possession or control of property, or

(4) in respect of a breach by the Crown of statutory duties, even though the common law presumption that the Crown is not bound by statute is still applicable unless excluded by the statutes concerned expressly or by necessary intendment.

On reflection it is a little difficult to understand quite what this section means, as it is hard to imagine the Crown committing any tort, except through a servant or agent, particularly since section 40 of the Act preserves the immunity of the Monarch personally from any liability in law. It is indeed possible that the true meaning of the section as enacted, though not necessarily as intended by the legislature, is to provide a general right of action in tort against the Crown wherever the Crown has been responsible for the commission of any tort whatever. But any further consideration of the section must be deferred until the reader had consulted more detailed works upon the subject.[1] The common law personal liability of Crown servants of course remains untouched in any way by the Act. Such servants are personally liable for any injuries they commit for which they are unable to produce legal authority.

The remaining sections of the Act provide for certain special matters either not covered by the two general sections or exceptional to them. There is no need to examine them fully here, but in particular it is enacted that the Crown is not liable for the death or personal injury of a member of the armed forces on duty caused by any other such member of the armed forces (section 10). As regards this latter situation, the Admiralty Board or a Secretary of State may, if satisfied of the facts, issue a certificate that the persons concerned were on duty as members of the armed forces, and this certificate is final and may not be questioned in any court of law. The Crown may now be ordered to produce documents relevant to any particular case (section 28), although the privilege to withhold such documents where a Minister certifies that their production might be injurious to the public interest is still

---

[1] See *e.g.* G. L. Williams, *Crown Proceedings* (1948); H. Street, *Governmental Liability* (1953); G. H. Treitel, "Crown Proceedings: Recent Developments", [1957] *Public Law* 321; and the textbooks and sourcebooks on administrative law.

left to the executive. "Crown privilege", as it is called, used to be accepted by the courts virtually without restriction, but in 1968 the House of Lords held that courts have the power to disallow any such claims of privilege, and to order the production of the documents concerned.[1] A court should not, however, order the production of Cabinet minutes, or of documents the disclosure of which would be contrary to national security.

Thus, although there are still exceptions and reservations, the Crown is now far nearer the position of a private contractor, employer or occupier of premises as far as litigation is concerned than it was before 1947. To this extent English law has approached more nearly to the concept of the rule of law favoured by Dicey, . and discussed above in Chapter 5.

B. *Indirect Remedies*

(1) *The prerogative orders*

Since the middle ages the superior courts of law (now the High Court in England) have possessed three methods of controlling the exercise of jurisdiction in inferior courts or bodies, and tribunals and inquiries of all kinds now come into the latter category. These methods of control were known as the prerogative writs, and their nature is essentially the same today, although their procedure was simplified by the Administration of Justice (Miscellaneous Provisions) Act, 1938, s. 7, so that they have now become prerogative orders. Each will be explained very shortly.

(a) *Certiorari.*—Any party who believes himself aggrieved by the proceedings of an administrative authority may apply to the High Court for a certiorari.

If any one of the alleged grounds for judicial control is proved to the satisfaction of the High Court (applications for any of the prerogative orders always being heard by a Divisional Court of the Queen's Bench Division), the proceeding below is quashed. Error of law on the face of the record of the inferior authority is no longer such a common ground for certiorari in practice as it was before direct appeals from most tribunals to the High Court on points of law were established by the Tribunals and Inquiries Act, 1958, (now 1971), but it remains important for the review of

---

[1] *Conway* v. *Rimmer*, [1968] 1 All E.R.874; [1968] A.C.910.

cases decided by tribunals, such as the National Insurance Commissioner, from which no such appeal yet lies. But it should be noted that no alternative decision on the merits is made by the High Court, in a certiorari case, thus distinguishing the effect of this remedy from that of appeal.

(*b*) *Prohibition.*—This order is similar in most respects to certiorari, except that its effect, if granted, is to prevent a case from being heard or continuing before, say, a tribunal, rather than to quash what has already taken place. Thus it is sought at an earlier stage in the proceedings before the tribunal, but the grounds for its issue are similar, even though it is rare, if possible at all, that an error of law can be alleged, because the record of the issue is not yet completed below.

(*c*) *Mandamus.*—Whereas the two previous orders are negative in effect, mandamus is positive, for if granted it has the effect of ordering the tribunal to do something, It may be sought, for example, where a tribunal has refused to hold a proper hearing, or where a Minister has failed to carry out a public duty or exercise a discretion entrusted to him.[1]

All three of these remedies are regarded as "last resort" remedies, for it is possible that a statute may have laid down a method of appeal from the particular tribunal concerned, in which case that course must be followed to the dissatisfaction of one of the parties before a prerogative order may be granted. No prerogative order may be granted along with any other remedy of a different kind, but any two or three of the prerogative orders may be obtained from the court at the same time in appropriate cases. Certain limitations upon their use should be noted, in that a certiorari may only be obtained within six months of the proceeding complained of (although there is no time limit for applications for prohibitions or mandamus), and a mandamus will not lie against the Crown or any servant of the Crown, to order him to perform any duty owed exclusively to the Crown, even though it will lie against an administrative tribunal. On the other hand certain limitations on the supervisory powers of the courts by means of certiorari and mandamus were relaxed by the Tribunals and Inquiries Act, 1958, (now 1971).

---

[1] *E.g.* in *Padfield* v. *Minister of Agriculture, Fisheries and Food*, [1968] 1 All E.R.694; [1964] A.C.997.

(2) Other indirect remedies

(a) Declaration.—A simple declaration of the law upon a particular point may sometimes be an appropriate remedy against an administrative authority. No declaration may be sought, however, unless the point at issue is a real, and not theoretical, one; and a possible drawback to the remedy is that there is no method whereby it may be enforced, since the issue before the court is not strictly a "live" dispute. All other judgments may always be enforced by attachment for contempt, but there is no direct method of coercing a party against whom a declaration has been obtained. It may be that disobedience would lead to a later direct action for damages or an injunction, in which the law would already have been decided, and only the facts would have to be proved. In any case it is possible to obtain a declaration in conjunction with some other positive remedy, such as an award of damages or an injunction, and there appears to be no record of a case in which a declaration has been disobeyed. But a court has refused a declaration where such a non-coercive remedy would be ineffective, as where the complaint was not that a tribunal had acted *ultra vires*, in which case its decision would be a nullity, but merely that it had made an error of law within the confines of its jurisdiction, which has been held to make the decision voidable.[1] It would not be possible for such a tribunal to reopen the matter unless its original decision had been *quashed*.

(b) Injunction.—This remedy has the effect of forbidding the doing of something, as being illegal. Thus it in many ways substantially resembles prohibition, but it is not used so often against administrative tribunals, and, like mandamus, it will not lie against the Crown. Its most common use in the field of administrative law is against so-called "domestic tribunals", such as disciplinary committees (*e.g.* of the Jockey Club), which are set up for internal purposes within a profession or a club, rather than by statute. Again, as with the declaration, an injunction may be obtained in conjunction with some other remedy, except one of the prerogative orders.

---

[1] *Punton* v. *Ministry of Pensions and National Insurance (No. 2)*, [1964] 1 All E.R.448; [1964] 1 W.L.R.226.

V. Extra-judicial Remedies

In the field of pure administration there has been a growing feeling that the citizen requires some further safeguard to his liberties and rights in addition to the traditional Parliamentary question and the doctrine of ministerial responsibility to Parliament. The Parliamentary Commissioner Act, 1967 was passed in response to this feeling, and it establishes for Great Britain a Parliamentary Commissioner for Administration modelled on the Scandinavian office of Ombudsman.[1] The Commissioner is appointed by the Crown and holds office until he is 65, being otherwise removable only in consequence of an address from both Houses of Parliament, so that his tenure of office is protected in the same way as that of the superior Judges. He may investigate any action taken by or on behalf of a Government Department or certain other listed authorities, if there is no court or tribunal in which such action may reasonably be challenged but his investigation may only be initiated where a complaint has first been made to him through an M.P. Cabinet papers are exempt from any investigation, but otherwise the Commissioner's powers to search and question are wide. He has no power to enforce any decision he may arrive at, but he must report his results to the M.P. and Government Department concerned, and may also report to Parliament.

Although the first two holders of this office have so far interpreted their powers somewhat restrictively, the Parliamentary Commissioner is a valuable aid for keeping the proper balance of power between the citizen and the state. A National Health Service Commissioner, operating on similar lines, has recently been appointed, and a Commission for Local Administration which would investigate complaints of maladministration by local authorities, is planned. The first Health Service Commissioner is Sir Alan Marre, who also currently holds the office of Parliamentary Commissioner. The appointment of Ombudsman-style tribunals to check on the investigation of complaints against the police is currently being considered by the Home Secretary.

---

[1] The first such office to be created in the Commonwealth was in New Zealand in 1962. A Parliamentary Commissioner was also established in Northern Ireland in 1969.

FURTHER READING

H. W. R. Wade, *Administrative Law* (3rd ed., 1971).

J. F. Garner, *Administrative Law* (3rd ed., 1970).

D. C. M. Yardley, *A Source Book of English Administrative Law* (2nd ed., (1970).

J. A. G. Griffith and H. Street, *Principles of Administrative Law* (4th ed., 1967).

S. A. de Smith, *Judicial Review of Administrative Action* (3rd ed., 1973).

B. Schwartz, *Introduction to American Administrative Law* (2nd ed., 1962).

The Annual Reports of the Council on Tribunals.

The Reports of the Parliamentary Commissioner for Administration.

CHAPTER 12

LOCAL GOVERNMENT

The machinery for the government of local areas throughout the United Kingdom is almost entirely separate from that of the national Government, though always subject to the overriding powers of Parliament by statute or, where appropriate, of the Central Government. It is of course possible and proper for the Government of the whole country to exercise such powers as it possesses by virtue of Acts of Parliament or the Royal Prerogative in such a way as to affect local areas of the Kingdom in various different ways. But, subject to such exercise of power, the different local authorities are independently empowered to carry out and enforce executive duties within their particular districts. They may also legislate upon certain matters within their jurisdiction and all these powers are derived either from Acts of Parliament or from Royal Charters granted under the Royal Prerogative.[1] The exercise of the Prerogative in this field is regulated by statute, and the powers of local authorities are mostly contained in the London Government Act, 1963, and the Local Government Act, 1972. It is our purpose in this chapter to outline the types of local authorities which exist at the present time, and their various powers. The authorities listed below are those which exist in England and Wales, all of which are under the general supervision of the Secretary of State for the Environment, although this does not mean that he necessarily wields great arbitrary powers over them. The local authorities in Northern Ireland are not dissimilar in the main, and elections for the recently reformed Northern Ireland district councils were first held in 1973. They are under the supervision of the Secretary of State for Northern Ireland. The authorities in Scotland, which have a different structure (stemming from the different legal system and history of the country), are supervised by the Secretary of State for Scotland.

---

[1] And see Chapters 3 and 10, *ante*.

t may be noted that, in Northern Ireland, elections both for the
district councils and for the Assembly, discussed in Chapter 7,
re held by proportional representation, *i.e.* members of political
parties are elected in similar proportion to that of the votes cast.
Elsewhere in the United Kingdom all elections are conducted
according to the principle that the winner is whichever candidate
eceives the most votes.

I. THE TYPES OF LOCAL AUTHORITIES

The local authorities of England and Wales may be divided up
s follows:

1) *The local authorities of London*

The local government organisation in the London area was
eorganised by the London Government Act, 1963. Greater
London consists of the City of London, the thirty-two London
Boroughs, the Inner Temple and the Middle Temple. Greater
London now includes areas which were previously parts of
urrounding counties, but it is possible that the Act of 1963 does
ot go far enough, in that it fails to take account of large areas in
urrounding counties where many working Londoners live. The
uthorities of Greater London are as follows:

(*a*) *The Greater London Council.* This consists of a chairman,
aldermen and councillors, though, under the terms of the Local
Government Act, 1972, aldermen are abolished with effect from
977. Councillors are elected every four years. The chairman
s elected annually by the council, and the aldermen have been
lected by the council for terms of six years, half of them re-
ring every third year. The G.L.C. is perhaps the most powerful
f all the local authorities in the country, because of the vast
opulation within London. It has extensive powers over
metropolitan roads, planning, reserve housing, main sewerage,
ewage disposal, fire protection, ambulances and civil defence. A
ommittee of the G.L.C., known as the Inner London Education
uthority, administers the education service within the area
ccupied by the twelve "Inner London Boroughs".

(*b*) *London Borough Councils.* There is one council for each of
he London Boroughs, and each consists of a mayor, aldermen
nd councillors, though the aldermen are to disappear in 1977.

The mayor is elected annually by the council, and the alder
men and councillors are elected in a similar way to those i
the G.L.C. The powers of these councils cover such subject
as local health, sanitation, the provision of public baths an
libraries, children, and the collection of rates, which are i
effect local taxes. The twenty "Outer London Boroughs" are als
education authorities.

(c) *The City of London Corporation.* This body corporate cam
into being as a result of prescription over a long period of histor
but its powers have been regulated from time to time by Roy
Charters and by statutes. It may be regarded as roughly of parall
status to the London Borough Councils, and its functions ar
exactly the same. The government of the corporation is carrie
on through three "Courts" or councils, the Court of Commo
Council, the Court of Common Hall and the Court of Aldermer
It is not necessary here to consider further their exact functions c
composition, but the various representatives who sit in thes
Courts are the Lord Mayor of London, aldermen, commo
councilmen, the two Sheriffs and certain liverymen of the ancier
City Companies of craftsmen and tradesmen.

(d) *The Benchers of the Inner and Middle Temples.* Certai
minor local government functions are still exercised by the bencher
of these two Inns of Court, and the London Government Act
1939 and 1963, recognise that the Temples are within Greate
London, but outside the City and the London Boroughs. This :
a traditional status, for which there appears to be no real leg
foundation, other than prescription or custom,[1] but it is of littl
importance in practice, as the inhabitants of the area are nearl
all barristers in their chambers, very few of whom actually resid
in the Temple.

In addition to the authorities so far listed, there are a number c
separate authorities administering services which, outside Londo
are often the concern of local authorities. These include th
Metropolitan Water Board, the Thames Conservancy, the Port c
London Authority, and the London Transport Board.

---

[1] But see Williamson, *The History of the Temple, London,* for furth
information.

) *Local authorities outside London*

Outside London the structure of local authorities is uniform and overned by the Local Government Act, 1972. The present authorities were elected for the first time in 1973, and took over their full powers on April 1st, 1974. In effect the country is for local government purposes covered by a three-tier system of authorities, governing respectively counties, districts and parishes. But six of the counties are designated as metropolitan counties, because they cover areas of the greatest concentration of population and industry, such as the West Midlands and Merseyside. In these counties there are metropolitan districts, the authorities for which have rather greater powers than those in non-metropolitan districts. The three types of authorities are as follows:

(*a*) *County councils*. Each council consists of a chairman and councillors, all of whom are elected for four years, and all of whom retire at the same time. The next election for these councils will be in the spring of 1977. Each council has a number of powers exercised concurrently with district councils, such as the control of museums and art galleries, swimming baths, parks and open spaces, tree preservation, and many aspects of town development. But the county council has exclusive powers over such matters as structure plans for the county, highways, traffic, consumer protection and refuse disposal. County councils outside metropolitan areas also have exclusive powers over the very important matters of education, youth employment, personal social services and libraries.

(*b*) *District councils*. Each county is divided into a number of districts, each of which has its own council, consisting of a chairman and councillors. Each member is elected for four years, but one-third of the council will retire every year, except for a year in which a county council election is to be held. As the first members of these councils were elected in 1973, it has been provided that further elections of one-third of each council shall take place in 1975, 1976 and 1978, *i.e.* in each of the four years after 1974, except for the year 1977 in which the next county council election will take place. Any district council or London Borough Council may, however, opt for the whole council to be elected together every four years, and the London Boroughs have so opted. As well as the powers exercised concurrently with county councils, district councils have exclusive powers over such matters as

housing, planning development control, building regulation
markets and fairs, local licensing, refuse collection, clean air an
home safety. Metropolitan district councils also have exclusiv
powers over education, youth employment, personal social service
and libraries.

(*c*) *Parish councils and meetings.* All parishes in rural areas hav
parish meetings, which consist of a chairman and all the loc
government electors of the parish, and which must meet at lea
once a year. Such parishes with a population of 300 or more mu
also have a parish council (and parishes with a population
under 300 may elect to have a parish council), consisting of
chairman, elected annually, and councillors, elected for four yea
and retiring in rotation. A council has slightly greater powers tha
a meeting, but the powers of each cover such subjects as th
maintenance and signposting of footpaths and bridleways, an
parks and open spaces.

In all these authorities, except parish meetings, members ar
directly elected by the people, and the abolition of aldermen i
the G.L.C. and the London Boroughs will complete this patter
for the whole country. But councils have the power to recognis
service to local government by conferring the title of "honorar
alderman" upon suitable persons. Non-elected members may b
co-opted to committees. Special provisions enable any distri
council for an area which was previously a borough by Roy
Charter to retain its previous status, together with the title
mayor for its chairman. Similarly a petition may be submitted, an
will be favourably considered, to enable any district to retain an
special distinction or title, such as "Royal Borough", "City
"Lord Mayor" or "Sheriff".

Of more fundamental importance, the Local Government Ac
1972 extends the right of the public and press to attend counc
meetings to meetings of all committees of local authoritie
Councillors now receive a taxable flat-rate attendance allowanc
when on council business. Local Government Boundary Commi
sions have also been set up on a permanent basis to review loc
government boundaries and electoral arrangements.

It will be seen from the above that the local administration
each part of England and Wales is accounted for by a greater an
a lesser authority, neither of which is a national body. But th

Central Government does have certain supervisory powers over these authorities, which are conferred by Act of Parliament. It is not necessary here to examine the supervisory powers closely, for they are of different kinds created under different statutes, but primarily this control exists because all local authorities receive financial grants from the Treasury to supplement rates levied and to pay for such local administration as cannot be afforded by the local funds. It is therefore easy to appreciate that the Government will only initiate or support legislation in Parliament to provide for such financial grants when the local authorities affected have behaved in a proper manner in the immediate past, and seem likely to continue to do so. Sometimes the Secretary of State is empowered to make discretionary grants or to supervise the local authorities in certain ways according to his discretion, and then the exercise of such discretion will depend even more upon the "good behaviour" of the authorities concerned. Further reform of the financing of local government is expected shortly, but in certain ways the 1972 Act has provided local authorities with greater financial freedom than hitherto. It can also be seen that, just as Parliament is able to control the functions and even the existence of local authorities by virtue of its legislative supremacy,[1] so it may also delegate powers of administration or legislation to the Central Government and to the local government authorities.[2] The powers of the latter are both administrative and legislative, with the restrictions discussed already in Chapter 10.

It is not proposed to discuss further in this chapter the powers of local authorities over the police, upon which the reader will find an account in Chapter 3 above. There is also no need to deal specifically with the powers to create committees or appoint officers (such as Chief Executive Officers), all of which depend on their governing legislation.

II. WHO ELECTS MEMBERS OF LOCAL AUTHORITIES?

Since the Representation of the People Act, 1949, the franchise for local government elections has been practically equated to that existing for Parliamentary elections, even though it is not quite identical. The right to vote is possessed by all British subjects or citizens of the Republic of Ireland of full age who are (1) not

---

[1] See Chapter 2, *ante.*
[2] See Chapters 10 and 11, *ante.*

subject to any legal incapacity,[1] and (2) either resident in the
area on the qualifying date,[2] or, if not so resident, who occupy as
owners or tenants any rateable land or premises in the area of the
yearly value of not less than £10. Thus there is an alternative
occupation qualification for those who cannot satisfy the residence
qualification. Peers also have the right to vote in local elections.

Since the local government reorganisation of the past few years,
party politics have come to play almost as great a part in local
government elections as they do in national elections, and most
candidates for election now stand as party candidates. In many
ways the growth of the party political element in local government is regrettable, since the problems for any administrative
sub-division of the country are practical everyday ones rather
than questions of national importance, and there are all too many
examples of experienced and hard-working local councillors who
lose their seats solely because of the temporary swing of the political
pendulum against their own party. But on the other hand social
policy is bound to play a certain part in the duties of such authorities, and there may be some advantages in groups of council
members having a worked-out and agreed policy on such issues.
Fortunately there is no record of grants to local authorities from the
Exchequer having been influenced to any great extent by the
political bias of the Central Government in relation to local
authorities dominated by members of their own or an opposition
party.

FURTHER READING

Sir W. Ivor Jennings, *Principles of Local Government Law* (4th ed.
by J. A. G. Griffith, 1960).
C. A. Cross, *Principles of Local Government Law* (4th ed., 1971).
W. E. Hart and W. O. Hart, *Introduction to the Law of Local Government
and Administration* (9th ed., by Sir W. O. Hart and J. F. Garner,
1973).
W. E. Jackson, *The Structure of Local Government in England and Wales*
(5th ed., 1966).
R. M. Jackson, *The Machinery of Local Government* (2nd ed., 1965).
P. W. Jackson, *Local Government* (2nd ed., 1970).
J. A. G. Griffith, *Central Departments and Local Authorities* (1967).
R. J. Buxton, *Local Government* (2nd ed., 1973).

---

[1] See Chapter 2, *ante*. The legal incapacities are the same as for national
elections, save that peers may vote in local elections.
[2] October 10th in each year, the annual register of electors being published
the following February 15th: Electoral Registers Act, 1953.

status now existing between the United Kingdom and the other full members, any such decision to revoke the common link of allegiance to the Crown, but still to remain a member of the Commonwealth, must be accepted by all the other members. On the analogy of a club with no specific rule for the alteration of its present rules, any one member would probably be able to black-ball another member which desired to alter its status yet again, but still remain a member.

The term "Dominion", which was used in the Statute of Westminster to denote the independent members of the Commonwealth, has now fallen out of use, because of the possible colonial ring in its sound. What would previously have been known as Dominions are now called full members or independent members of the Commonwealth.

It seems that the granting of independence by the United Kingdom to a country which previously possessed the status of, for example, a colony is a question for the United Kingdom Government and Parliament alone.[1] But the approval of all the existing independent members must be obtained before the newly independent nation may take its place in the Commonwealth as an equal with the existing members.[2] The same principle will apply in the case of the granting of independence to any of their dependencies by other full members of the Commonwealth. Australia and New Zealand, for example, have a number of dependencies which may be affected in this way. The full members of the Commonwealth which have attained their status since 1931 (and in fact all of them since the Second World War), and which have joined the "Club" of the United Kingdom, Canada, Australia and New Zealand, are India, Sri Lanka (formerly Ceylon),

---

[1] But see the section of this chapter dealing with associated states, *post.* Rhodesia made a unilateral declaration of independence in 1965, but this has not been recognised by the United Kingdom or by other members of the Commonwealth. In 1970 Rhodesia also purported to become a republic.

[2] See the statement of Mr. (later Sir) Winston Churchill to the House of Commons on June 16th, 1952, 502 H.C.Deb.778; also S. A. de Smith, "The Independence of Ghana", (1957) 20 *Modern Law Review* 347, at pp. 352–354. It may be noted that at the time of the passage of the Ghana Independence Act, 1957, there was some apprehension that South Africa might oppose the new nation's full membership of the Commonwealth because of the colour question, but these fears proved groundless. Further difficulties over racial problems were averted for the time being by South Africa's withdrawal from the Commonwealth in 1961.

Ghana, Malaysia, Cyprus, Nigeria, Sierra Leone, Western Samoa, Jamaica, Trinidad and Tobago, Uganda, Singapore, Kenya, Tanzania, Malawi, Malta, Zambia, the Gambia, Guyana, Botswana, Lesotho, Barbados, Mauritius, Swaziland, Tonga, Fiji, Bangladesh, the Bahamas, and Grenada.[1] It is possible that a few more dependencies will achieve this status before the list can be regarded as complete. The indepedent republic of Nauru was, in 1968, granted "special membership" of the Commonwealth. This includes the same rights to participate in Commonwealth affairs as other independent members, but not the right to be represented at meetings of Commonwealth heads of government. It is unecessary, for the purposes of an introductory book restricted to British consitutional law, to embark upon a discussion of the detailed constitutional organisation of any of these independent members of the Commonwealth, though it may be noted that, in distinction from the United Kingdom, the Constitutions of these countries are, with the partial exception of New Zealand, to be found in specific constitutional documents. This is logical, for whereas the Constitution of the United Kingdom grew up with the gradual development of the free and independent country itself, these other countries are, so to speak, new creations, and have had no time in which to "evolve" Constitutions. But it may be borne in mind that India, Sri Lanka, Ghana, Cyprus, Nigeria, Sierra Leone, Uganda, Singapore, Kenya, Tanzania, Malawi, Zambia, the Gambia, Guyana, Botswana and Bangladesh are republics, and have thus renounced allegiance to the Crown, though their Constitutions either provide or impliedly recognise that the United Kingdom Monarch is to be recognised as symbolic Head of the Commonwealth. Lesotho has its Paramount Chief as Head of State; Swaziland and Tonga have their own Kings; and Malaysia and Western Samoa maintain their own special forms of an elected monarchy. Each has therefore renounced allegiance to the Crown, but still recognises the British Monarch as the Head of the Commonwealth. It is doubtful whether this title means anything in reality. Canada, Cyprus, Ghana, India, Sri Lanka, Guyana, Sierra Leone, Singapore, Nigeria, Tanzania and Zambia have all abolished the right of appeal from their courts to the Privy Council. The possibility of such appeals from

---

[1] Pakistan, which was a member, left the Commonwealth in 1972.

Kenya, the Gambia, Malawi and Uganda is greatly reduced. Australian appeals lie to the Privy Council only in cases where the High Court has already heard an appeal from a State Supreme Court which does not involve federal jurisdiction, or the interpretation or application of the Australian Constitution or of a federal law. It is among the aims of the present Australian Government to abolish this right of appeal to the Privy Council.

In a world of growing nationalism the changes in structure and pattern of the Commonwealth come thick and fast; so much so, indeed, that no textbook writer could ever hope to remain up-to-date at the time of publication of his work. The Commonwealth is becoming more and more flexible, and it is clear that any innovation is possible, provided the existing full members are prepared to agree to it. Thus, quite apart from the admission of republics to the Commonwealth, and the diminishing jurisdiction of the Judicial Committee of the Privy Council, one might point, for example, to the admission of Cyprus in 1961, the year after its attainment of independence, for an experimental period of five years—a period which Cyprus itself, after a vote in its House of Representatives, had stipulated in its application to join the Commonwealth, and which has since been prolonged. For the future it is possible that even purely foreign countries, with no former links with the Commonwealth at all, might be admitted, should they apply. Perhaps also the very size of the independent Commonwealth may cause the introduction of some form of regional grouping for certain purposes. The entry of the United Kingdom to the European Community in 1973, mentioned in Chapter 2, might eventually have some effect upon Commonwealth relations and structure, though it is hard as yet to see what that effect might be. Some thinkers believe that the Commonwealth is now growing so big that it will cease to be effective for any purpose, save in its common use of the English language and its sharing of the British educational system and Parliamentary institutions. Obviously the links between the United Kingdom and the older members, Australia, New Zealand and Canada, must be to some extent closer than between any of these countries and the other members of the Commonwealth, partly because of blood relationship and partly because the British were never conquerors in the three older countries (except as far as the French Canadians and Maoris were concerned). But there is no sign as yet that the Asian and African members wish to disband the Commonwealth, or even to weaken it appreciably.

Two odd and perhaps anomalous legal links between the United Kingdom and Canada, and the United Kingdom and Australia may be noted here. Canada and Australia are federations, that is, the countries are organised with both central (or national) and provincial or State legislatures, Governments and courts, the powers of each being carefully laid down in the Constitution of each country.

Specific powers in Canada are vested in the provincial authorities, and the residue of power remains in the federal Parliament and Government. Until 1949 all constitutional changes had to be brought about by statutes of the United Kingdom Parliament, but by the British North America (No. 2) Act of that year the Constitution may now be amended by ordinary federal legislation, except as regards:

(1) matters assigned exclusively to the provincial legislatures;
(2) the rights or privileges of provincial legislatures or Governments;
(3) rights relating to schools and the use of the English and French languages; and
(4) the requirements that the federal Parliament should meet at least once a year, and that no House of Commons should continue for more than five years (except "in time of real or apprehended war, invasion or insurrection", when the House may continue to sit, provided no more than one-third of its members oppose the proposal).

These provisions are of course to protect the rights of the Provinces against federal pressure, but the United Kingdom Parliament might find itself in an awkward position if asked by the federal authorities to initiate amending legislation on one of these four matters despite the active opposition of one of the Provinces. Fortunately the position has never yet arisen, but it is not clear what the duty of the United Kingdom Parliament would be. It should be noted that the Canadian Parliament, in view of these restrictions upon the power of purely internal constitutional change, is still not entirely a sovereign Parliament, even though Canada itself is an independent member of the Commonwealth and is a sovereign state in international law. The "oldest Dominion" must in reality be regarded as quite independent, and there is no doubt such jurisdiction as is still retained by the Parliament at Westminster over Canadian constitutional change will be abandoned when the Canadian authorities so demand. An amendment to the Canadian Constitution to this effect is now pending, for in 1964 the Canadian Minister of Justice and the Attorneys-General of all the Provinces reached agreement upon a process whereby all future Canadian constitutional amendments should be made in Canada only. As soon as final approval for this draft amendment is obtained from all the provincial premiers and legislatures, it will be submitted to the United Kingdom Parliament. Once passed, the Act will be the last United Kingdom Act amending the Canadian Constitution.

The Commonwealth of Australia is a federation of six States, not Provinces. Its Constitution is contained in section 9 of the Commonwealth of Australia Constitution Act, 1900, as amended from time to time, and the salient difference between this federation and that of Canada is that the Australian federation is similar to the model of the United States of America, conferring specific powers upon the federation, whilst the residue of power remains with the States, and not with the centre. It is perhaps partly for this reason and partly because of the absence of any racial or religious problems in Australia that there was never any need for the United Kingdom Parliament to retain any legislative powers over the federation, and constitutional change is a purely internal process. Curiously enough, the State legislatures, as opposed to the federal Parliament, are still subject to the Colonial Laws Validity Act, 1865, as they are unaffected by the Statute of Westminister, 1931. This means that any legislation of a State legislature which is repugnant to an Act of the United Kingdom Parliament extending to that State shall be void. This may strictly be a legal limitation upon Australian legislative sovereignty, but even so it is not a limitation upon the *federation*, which is the state for the purposes of international law; and it should be emphasised that no United Kingdom Parliament would ever attempt to retain this control over the State legislatures if the latter should wish it to be removed. There is also some doubt whether the Commonwealth Parliament has the power to repeal or alter the first eight sections of the Commonwealth of Australia Constitution Act, 1900, concerning the position of Australia as a federation under the Crown, in view of the fact that the Constitution itself is only contained in section 9 of the Act, and that section 128 of the Constitution contains the mode of altering only the Constitution. No method of altering the first eight sections of the Act is mentioned in the statute itself, and thus it may be that an Act of the United Kingdom Parliament would be required to effect any change in or repeal of those sections. Such an Act would presumably be passed if ever requested by the Australian authorities. The Australian Government in 1973 opened negotiations with the United Kingdom for removal of all remaining technical legal powers possessed by the United Kingdom over Australia. There appears to be some opposition from the States to this proposal, and it remains to be seen what the outcome will be.

These technical fetters upon the Canadian Parliament and upon Australia are more illusory than real, and it would be hard to imagine the United Kingdom Government or Parliament ever wishing to interfere in any serious way with Canadian or Australian affairs. Nevertheless it is very doubtful whether any new independent member of the Commonwealth would ever wish so to dovetail its Constitution with the powers of the United Kingdom Parliament.[1]

In 1965 a Commonwealth Secretariat was established to distribute factual information to member countries, to promote Commonwealth links, and to co-ordinate preparations for meeting of Commonwealth Ministers. The first Secretary-General is a Canadian, and the Secretariat is based at Marlborough House, London.

III. Other Members of the Commonwealth which are not yet Independent

The so-called Imperialist aims of the nineteenth century have disappeared, and the intentions of all United Kingdom Governments in recent years have been to implement as far as possible the almost uniform desire of dependent peoples under the Crown for self-government. The achievement of this aim must in any case be a comparatively slow process, as some countries are not yet

---

[1] The military bases over which the United Kingdom has retained sovereignty in the island of Cyprus, and other military agreements with various Commonwealth countries, are in no way legal fetters upon the independence of those countries.

ready to be solely responsible for their own affairs. Furthermore, the aim may not be entirely possible of achievement in the long run for certain small countries which can never be economically self-supporting. It is of great interest to find the recent development of associate status within the Commonwealth, for this may provide the ideal solution for such small countries. The total population of the remaining dependent territories does not exceed five millions, and about four millions of these are in Hong Kong, where there are special reasons why the inhabitants do not at present desire any significant alteration in their colonial status.

In this short section we shall merely outline the various types of non-independent countries within the Commonwealth, without attempting to list all the individual territories concerned. The great majority of these countries are subject in some respect to United Kingdom sovereignty, but some are under the control of other independent Commonwealth countries, as has already been mentioned earlier in this chapter. It is not part of our present purpose to relate how the various territories concerned came to have their present status.

A. *Associate States*

It will be recalled from Chapter 7 that the Isle of Man and the Channel Islands are not strictly speaking part of the United Kingdom. For practical and international purposes they are grouped together with the United Kingdom as one independent member of the Commonwealth, though they really occupy a position partly independent and partly subordinate to the United Kingdom Parliament. In the second edition of this book it was suggested that this kind of association could be used as a basis for settling the future of small dependencies which could not, for various reasons, contemplate full independence. The settlement of the future of the Leeward and Windward Islands had given particular difficulty, but agreement for a kind of associate status was reached in 1966, and brought into effect by the West Indies Act, 1967, which conferred the new status upon Antigua, Dominica, St. Christopher-Nevis-Anguilla and St. Lucia. St. Vincent became an associated state in 1969. Grenada was an associated state from 1967 till full independence was attained in 1974.

Associate states have full control over their internal affairs, and they have the power by constitutional amendment to become fully independent, and thus to end their association with the United Kingdom at any time without further recourse to the United Kingdom Government or Parliament. The British Government retains responsibility for external affairs and the defence of each state, but otherwise the United Kingdom has no power to legislate for such a state or to conduct its affairs. Common citizenship with the United Kingdom is retained. A regional High Court and Court of Appeal for the West Indies has been set up

The 1968 Constitution for Gibraltar bears a close resemblance to some of these arrangements. In 1965 the Cook Islands became an associated state of New Zealand.

B. *Colonies*

A colony is any part of the dominions of the Crown which is not yet an independent member of the Commonwealth. The Isle of Man, the Channel Islands, the associate states, the Canadian Provinces and the Australian States are, however, excepted from this category. Direct allegiance is owed to the Crown. All persons born in British colonies are automatically British subjects and citizens of the United Kingdom and colonies. The Constitutions of colonies are provided either by Acts of Parliament or, more usually, by Orders in Council or Letters Patent, and the powers and privileges of colonies vary greatly with the local conditions educational progress etc. Thus a few colonies may still be administered directly from the United Kingdom, but the majority have their own legislative assemblies, of different degrees of representative character, and a few are almost entirely, or even completely, self-governing for internal affairs. All colonies have Governors who represent the Crown. As examples of colonies not yet very advanced in the progress towards self-government may be taken Hong Kong, the Pitcairn Islands, the British Antarctic Territory and Tristan da Cunha, whereas at the other end of the scale is Bermuda. Hong Kong is the only remaining territory to retain the title of Crown Colony.

C. *Protectorates*

Protectorates are territories under the protection of the Crown although they are not strictly British territory or part of the dominions of the Crown. But the Crown is responsible for their foreign affairs. Internally they are administered under British supervision of varying degrees of strictness by their native rulers, or else in a way very similar to those of colonies. The authority for the supervisory powers of the United Kingdom or of any other independent member of the Commonwealth came originally from treaties entered into with the native rulers, but it now derives both from the Royal Prerogative and from the Foreign Jurisdiction Act, 1890. The inhabitants of protectorates are not British subjects, but enjoy the status of British protected persons, who have certain advantages over aliens in British constitutional law. The only protectorate at present is that of the British Solomon Islands.

D. *Protected States*

Protected states are countries which are independent of the Crown internally, for they possess an organised form of government, but which have their external relations controlled entirely by the Crown. In all other ways they resemble protectorates, the rights which have been acquired by the Crown having accrued as a result of treaties. The only remaining protected state is Brunei.

E. *Trust Territories*

Trust territories (formerly League of Nations mandated territories) are administered by the Crown under the terms of the International Trusteeship system organised by the United Nations. The independent members of the Commonwealth are among a number of countries to which this type of trusteeship has been given. Internally and externally the territories are controlled by the trustee power, but reports must be submitted from time to time to the General Assembly of the United Nations and the Trusteeship Council, which will have an influence over the gradual development of the territories. No trust territories are part of the dominions of the Crown, but their inhabitants enjoy the status of British protected persons.

With the independence of Tanganyika in December 1961 the United Kingdom's present direct trusteeship responsibilities came to an end, though it is always possible for them to arise again at the behest of the United Nations. Its indirect responsibilities ended with Nauru's independence, granted in 1968. New Guinea, however, remains a trust territory administered by

Australia, although independence in conjunction with Papua i
imminent.

IV. THE PLACE OF THE COMMONWEALTH IN
BRITISH CONSTITUTIONAL LAW

There is no attempt in this book to give an account, howeve:
short, of the constitutional laws of those countries outside the
United Kingdom which are also members in some way of the
wider Commonwealth. It may therefore be asked why any mentior
of the Commonwealth should appear at all in the present volume
which is devoted to the constitutional laws of the United Kingdom
The answer is that British constitutional law is affected by the
relationship of the mother country with the other members of the
Commonwealth, and therefore it is our final task in this book to
indicate briefly the ways in which the law is so affected. This may
probably best be done in summary form, in view of the informa
tion which has already been given in the foregoing pages of the
present chapter.

(1) *The Crown and allegiance*

It used to be thought that the citizens of all independent membe
states of the Commonwealth must owe allegiance to the Crown
but the existence today of republics within the Commonwealtl
has disproved this theory. Yet common allegiance to the Crowr
by all member countries of the Commonwealth, other than the
independent republics, Lesotho, Swaziland, Malaysia, Tonga
Western Samoa, protectorates, protected states and trust territories
is still an important link, even if the concept of the Crown itself is o
a somewhat nebulous quality in this sphere, depending a great dea
upon a slightly illogical emotionalism. Even with the republics and
the separate monarchies the British Monarch remains as the symbc
of the unity of the Commonwealth, for those countries recognise hir
as Head of the Commonwealth. Among the more real results of th
allegiance owed to the Crown is the common British nationalit
conferred by United Kingdom law, even though British subject
now also enjoy citizenship of their own independent country o
of the United Kingdom and colonies, as has been seen above i
Chapter 8.[1] The citizens of protectorates, protected states an

---

[1] This British nationality has been abolished by the republics as far as the
own citizens are concerned.

trust territories, though not British subjects, enjoy the status of British protected persons.

(2) *Power over non-independent members of the Commonwealth*

The considerable power wielded by the United Kingdom or by other independent members of the Commonwealth over most non-independent members is very important for all members, as including an ability to control the destiny of peoples who are not inhabitants of the British Isles. As has been seen already in Chapters 2, 3 and 10, all such powers stem either from Acts of Parliament or from the Royal Prerogative.

(3) *Other links between independent members of the Commonwealth*

There are a number of loose links between full members, all of which could be broken at any time by any member acting unilaterally, but it is realised that there is much advantage to be gained from keeping the links. Thus there exist certain reciprocal trading and economic advantages, which are hardly within the scope of this volume. It is customary to enter into agreements with each other of a rather more informal nature than treaties. Conferences of Commonwealth Prime Ministers are normally held every year or so to discuss mutual problems; indeed, consultation at all levels on many subjects probably provides the most important Commonwealth link of all. High Commissioners are usually exchanged by the full members, rather than ambassadors, although their powers and status (as regards diplomatic immunity etc.) are similar. The right of appeal from the courts of all member countries to the Judicial Committee of the Privy Council has already been abolished by many independent members, but it still remains for those others which wish to retain it.

The Statute of Westminster, 1931, which has been discussed earlier, is particularly important. It expressly applied to, and was later accepted by legislative Acts in, the older independent members of the Commonwealth, and its substantive provisions have been written into the Independence Acts or the Constitutions of the post-war independent members. The provisions of the Statute lay down not only the final recognition that all independent members have complete legislative independence for internal and external matters, but also the only way in which the United Kingdom Parliament may still legislate in such a way as to alter the law in any other independent member of the Commonwealth.

Section 4 provides: "No Act of Parliament of the United Kingdom passed after the commencement of this Act shall extend, or be deemed to extend, to a Dominion as part of the law of that Dominion unless it is expressly declared in that Act that the Dominion has requested, and consented to, the enactment thereof." In view of the strictly sovereign legislative power of the United Kingdom Parliament, discussed above in Chapter 2, it would be possible for this section to be repealed expressly, or even by implication, so far as United Kingdom law *only* is concerned, at any time by another Act passed in the usual way, but, as Lord Sankey L.C. once said: "that is theory and has no relation to realities".[1] It would be unthinkable that any future Parliament should attempt to alter this provision without the requisite "request" and "consent". And in any case, regardless of English law, the law of, say, Australia would not be changed as far as Australia itself was concerned by a United Kingdom Act, unless there had been the requisite "request" and "consent".[2]

(4) *The adoption of British institutions*

It is noteworthy that the executive, legislative and judicial functions in most full member countries have often followed the model of the United Kingdom, at least in the first instance. There are modifications in all countries, but the basic plan is frequently similar. The modifications may well be quite extensive and there has been a trend in the African and Asian countries towards a Constitution with a Presidential system on the United States model, instead of a Parliamentary system. But even those Commonwealth countries with this type of Constitution have managed to work into their systems many British-type institutions. The transfer of British institutions to other Commonwealth countries may well prove to be the greatest contribution of the United Kingdom to any of these countries. Electoral systems vary but the Parliamentary systems are often similar. Even the much criticised House of Lords is not shunned in all aspects, for where

---

[1] *British Coal Corporation* v. *R.*, [1935] A.C.500, at p. 520; [1935] All E.R Rep. 139, at p. 146.

[2] See H. R. Gray, "The Sovereignty of the Imperial Parliament" (1960), 2 *Modern Law Review* 647.

[3] Mr. S. Namasivayam, in *Parliamentary Government on Ceylon, 1948–195* (1959), believes that the British-type Constitution of Ceylon is likely to b retained.

upper Houses have been created their membership is usually of a more long term nature than that of the lower House, and in Canada membership of the Senate is for life. Again, it is normal for Ministers in all member countries to be members of the legislature, thus following the British pattern of responsibility to Parliament, and eschewing the American type of separation of powers, discussed in Chapter 6.

(5) *Miscellaneous*

Among other lesser matters may be noticed the powers retained by the United Kingdom Parliament over constitutional change in Canada and over the State legislatures in Australia, though it must be re-emphasised that such powers will always be removed if the Canadian or Australian authorities wish them to be. Finally, any citizens of independent Commonwealth countries who are also United Kingdom peers, and who wish to sit in the House of Lords in Westminster, may do so. In recent years the former Prime Ministers of Australia, Viscount Bruce of Melbourne, and of the Central African Federation of Rhodesia and Nyasaland, Lord Malvern, have done so, though the latter was in any case a native of England. Lord Casey, a former Australian Minister for External Affairs, became a life peer, having been so created under the Life Peerages Act, 1958.[1] Though a small matter, it may indicate the elasticity and the strength of the Commonwealth, and the relations between its members.

FURTHER READING

Sir W. Ivor Jennings, *Constitutional Laws of the Commonwealth*, Vol. I: The Monarchies (3rd ed., 1957).
K. C. Wheare, *The Constitutional Structure of the Commonwealth* (1960).
The British Commonwealth: The Development of its Laws and Constitutions series. 14 Vols.
S. A. de Smith, *The New Commonwealth and its Constitutions* (1964).
The Annual Survey of Commonwealth Law.
D. C. M. Yardley, "Commonwealth Membership: its Present and Future", (1960) XIII *Parliamentary Affairs* 346.

---

[1] See Chapter 2, *ante.*

INDEX

A

ACTS OF PARLIAMENT
generally, 14. *And see* BILL,
PARLIAMENT

ADMINISTRATIVE LAW
generally, 105

ADMINISTRATIVE TRIBUNALS
appeals from, 120
to High Court, 121
appellate tribunals, 121
Committee on, 117
Council on, 120
criticisms, 118
damages, actions for, 124
Franks Committee, 118
generally, 117, 120
judicial control of, 122
necessity of, 117
reforms, 120
remedies against, 124 *et seq.*
Tribunals and Inquiries Act, 118
types, 119

AFFRAY
common law offence, 90

ALIENS
arrest and imprisonment of, 98
civic rights, 98
internment and deportation, 98
temporary allegiance owed by, 96

ALLEGIANCE
Crown, to, 96

APPEAL
High Court of Justice, 55
House of Lords, 58

APPELLATE TRIBUNALS
Tribunals and Inquiries Act, 120

ARMED FORCES
executive, 43
prerogative power of Crown, under,
126

ARREST
issue of warrant, 83
without warrant, 83

ASSEMBLY
incursions upon freedom of, 89 *et
seq.*

ATTORNEY-GENERAL
appointment and duties, 41

AUSTRALIA
constitution and government, 145

B

BILL
generally, 14
government, what is, 14
hybrid, 18
money, 19
private, 17
public, 15
readings, 15
Royal Assent to, 17, 18

BILL OF RIGHTS 1689
significance, 29

BREAST LAW
Isle of Man, 76

BRITISH NATIONALITY
Commonwealth, 150

BRITISH SUBJECT
meaning, 96

BYE-LAWS
local authority, of, 109
public corporation, of, 109

C

CABINET
generally, 40

CANADA
constitution, generally, 144

CENTRAL CRIMINAL COURT
crown court for London, 58

CERTIORARI
application for, 127

CHANCERY DIVISION
High Court of Justice, 55

CHANNEL ISLANDS
legislation and laws, 77